D0623774

TRADITIONS OF
AMERICAN
EDUCATION

TRADITIONS OF AMERICAN EDUCATION

LAWRENCE A. CREMIN

BASIC BOOKS, INC., PUBLISHERS

NEW YORK

The Merle Curti Lectures
University of Wisconsin
March, 1976

Library of Congress Cataloging in Publication Data

Cremin, Lawrence Arthur, 1925–
  Traditions of American education.

  Includes index.
  1. Education—United States—History. 2. Education—
Philosophy. I. Title.
LA205.C67   370'.973   76–43456
ISBN: 0–465–08685–3

CONTENTS

PREFACE

TO HAVE BEEN INVITED by the University of Wisconsin
to inaugurate the Merle Curti Lectures is one of the loveliest
honors that has come to me, and I am profoundly grateful.
The occasion affords me the opportunity to acknowledge on
behalf of an entire generation of American historians the debt
we owe Merle Curti for the inspiration and example of his
scholarship. And it gives me the chance to acknowledge as
well the debt I owe him personally for his encouragement, his
counsel, and his generosity over the years, and, most treasured
of all, for the gift of his friendship.

The opportunity to deliver the lectures came at a propitious
time in the course of my own scholarship, namely, the mid-
point of my efforts on a three-volume comprehensive history
of American education. Indeed, the lecture committee invited

me quite explicitly to use the occasion to discuss aspects of my work in progress. As a result, the first lecture, dealing with the period from the beginnings of colonization to the achievement of independence, is derived essentially from *American Education: The Colonial Experience*, which was published in 1970. My theme there is the successful transplantation of European educational institutions to the New World and their gradual modification under novel conditions. The second lecture, dealing with the first century of nationhood, is drawn from *American Education: The National Experience*, which has been fully drafted but not yet published. My theme there is the development of an authentic American vernacular in education, expressly intended to advance a popular *paideia* compounded of democratic hopes, evangelical pieties, and millennial expectations. And the third lecture, dealing with the period since Reconstruction, is based on *American Education: The Metropolitan Experience*, which has been substantially sketched but not yet fully drafted. My theme there is the transformation and proliferation of American educative agencies under the influence of industrialization, urbanization, technological innovation, and transnational expansion.

As in the larger work, I have defined education broadly, as the deliberate, systematic, and sustained effort to transmit, evoke, or acquire knowledge, attitudes, values, skills, or sensibilities, as well as any outcomes of that effort. And I have given particular attention in the lectures to the changing configurations of education at different times in American history and to the various ways in which individuals have interacted with those configurations. The more general theory underly-

Preface

ing all this is explicated in the note on problematics and
sources appended to the lectures and is further elaborated in
Public Education, which may be regarded as a companion to
the present volume.

I should like to state my gratitude to H. Edwin Young,
Chancellor of the University of Wisconsin at Madison, to
David Fellman, Theodore S. Hamerow, Jurgen Herbst, Carl
F. Kaestle, and Stanley I. Kutler, and to Merle Curti himself,
for their gracious hospitality during my stay at the University
in March of 1976. I should also like to acknowledge the gener-
ous assistance of Ellen Condliffe Lagemann, Steven L.
Schlossman, Judith Suratt, and Toni Thalenberg in the research on which the lectures are based and in the preparation
of the lectures for publication. And I should like finally to ex-
press my appreciation to the Carnegie Corporation of New
York for its continuing encouragement and support of my
scholarly endeavors.

L.A.C.

THE COLONIAL
EXPERIENCE:
1607–1783

THE SETTLEMENT of America, it has been said, had its origins in the unsettlement of Europe—in that vast and pervasive upheaval that scholars have come to call "the general crisis of the seventeenth century." The elements of the crisis are well known: the dissolution of the feudal economy and the rise of mercantile capitalism; the intellectual turbulence occasioned by the Renaissance and Reformation; the turmoil of the Thirty Years' War and the political rebellions that erupted almost simultaneously in a half-dozen different countries. "These days are days of shaking . . . ," the English preacher Jeremiah Whittaker lamented to the House of Commons during the winter of 1642–1643, "and this shaking is universal:

the Palatinate, Bohemia, Germania, Catalonia, Portugal, Ireland, England." [1]

Whittaker had every reason to talk of shaking, for England itself was in the throes of a civil war. But the sources of the shaking lay far deeper than the immediacies of that particular conflict. For almost a century, the effects of population growth, land speculation, social mobility, and religious strife had combined to rock the very foundations of English belief and custom. And popular malaise had only been exacerbated by disturbing reports of new planets in the heavens and new continents beyond the seas. Somehow, millennial hopes had linked with grim forebodings to portend that, whatever happened, nothing would ever be the same again. The result was a generation of "vexed and troubled Englishmen," of whom an unprecedented number simply decided to leave the country. A few crossed the Channel to France, Holland, and the Palatinate, where they eventually merged with the native populations. More crossed the Irish Sea to Ulster. But by far the greatest number crossed the Atlantic to America, establishing themselves there in a chain of settlements that stretched some thirty-six hundred miles, from Newfoundland on the north to Guiana on the Spanish Main. In the process, an empire came into being. [2]

Now, it is this fact of empire that holds the key to the dynamics of early American education. For one thing, the North American continent was neither empty nor virgin at the time

[1] Whittaker's lamentation is given in H. R. Trevor-Roper, "The General Crisis of the Seventeenth Century," in Trevor Astin, ed., *Crisis in Europe, 1560–1660* (London: Routledge & Kegan Paul, 1965), p. 59.

[2] Carl Bridenbaugh, *Vexed and Troubled Englishmen, 1590–1642* (New York: Oxford University Press, 1968).

of European settlement; it had been populated for centuries by a variety of Indian peoples, who had developed their own historic civilizations based on different combinations of hunting, fishing, mining, and agriculture. Thus, the initial reality of American education was the experience of culture contact. Whether the Europeans ended up enslaving the Indians, or dispersing them, or living side by side with them, they inevitably taught them and learned from them. And, while the literary sources on which historians have traditionally relied make much of the Europeans bringing the gospel to the heathen, it is well to remember that the heathen brought maize to the Europeans, along with much else by way of knowledge, skill, and wisdom that in the end may actually have enabled the Europeans to survive.

Then, too, quite apart from the Indians, the very notion of empire embodied an inescapable commitment to education. However the metropolis conceived of its colonies—as exploitative manufactories, or trading centers, or missionary outposts, or metropolitan exurbs—the metropolis became increasingly dependent upon education to nurture the discipline, the loyalty, and the expertise that were vital to the metropolitan-colonial relationship. In enforcing mercantilist policy, raw power and promised reward could go only so far—how many times, after all, could one proclaim that he who does not work shall not eat? Persuasion and the habits born of persuasion had to prevail. In the long run, it was easier to teach the reciprocal duties of king and commoner, the indissoluble ties of colony and mother-country, and the ultimate value of contentment.

Of course, the English were not the only people to colonize

North America during the sixteenth and seventeenth centuries. The Spanish established St. Augustine as early as 1565; the French planted permanent settlements in Acadia and Quebec in 1605 and 1608; the Dutch established New Amsterdam on the Hudson in 1624; and the Swedes founded New Sweden along the banks of the Delaware in 1638. And, beyond these organized quasi-governmental ventures, there were scattered groups of Spanish and Portuguese Jews, Scottish Presbyterians, and German sectarians who came on their own, and growing numbers of blacks who were brought forcibly to be sold into slavery. Obviously, the experience of culture contact went far beyond relationships between Europeans and Indians, it was of the essence in relationships between one group of Europeans and another. Whatever the burdens colonization itself might have placed on education, those burdens were only heightened by the presence of rival colonizers. We see the process at work in the seventeenth-century competition between the Dutch and the English in New York, and we see it too in the eighteenth-century competition between the French and the English in the region of the St. Lawrence. The Intercolonial Wars were cultural as well as military conflicts, with the loyalty of large numbers of Indians and whites very much at stake.

In the end, English culture triumphed, and with it English law, English language, and English custom. And that triumph, I would suggest, was decisive in the development of early American education. On the one hand, it testified to the extraordinary effectiveness of English educational endeavor, and, on the other hand, it set the pattern of much that would come later. To argue thus is not to deny that the English enjoyed considerable advantage in numbers, wealth, and colonial organization—after all, there were more Englishmen to begin with and they did prevail militarily—it is merely to assert that education had contributed to the victory.

How, then, do we explain this remarkable effectiveness of Anglo-American educational effort? I believe it derived from four sources. First, England itself had undergone a phenomenal educational development during the Tudor and early Stuart eras. There had been a revival of the ancient prophetic function within the Anglican church, with the Bible made widely available to the laity and the priesthood charged with the systematic exegesis of its teachings. Under the various statutes of supremacy and uniformity, a vast system of universal compulsory education had grown up, centered in the parish churches, controlled by the Crown and its official ecclesiastical representatives, conducted by an orthodox and closely supervised clergy, and concentrating on a curriculum consisting of the Bible and the Book of Common Prayer (which included an authorized catechism, an authorized book of homilies, and an authorized primer). There had been a contemporary expansion and revitalization of schooling, sparked by the humanists and assisted by a massive infusion of gifts from merchant and gentry families, and there had been a concomitant quickening of Oxford, Cambridge, and the Inns of Court, as new colleges were founded, new social groups gained access, and new subjects of study made their way into the curriculum. There had been a rapid extension of printing that, even under the most stringent royal control, had radically

7

increased the availability of knowledge and opinion of every variety, including some varieties that the authorities wished to proscribe. And there had been a succession of parliamentary acts requiring that every individual live within the discipline of some family or surrogate family and enjoining all families to see to the proper religious and vocational training of their members. The result was that the English had already had considerable experience with the political and social uses of education by the time of settlement and had worked out a fairly efficient organizational technology for delivering educational services on an unprecedented scale. And it was the Puritans, incidentally, who were to constitute such a significant proportion of the migrants, who had developed to the greatest degree both the readiness to use education for social purposes and the technology for doing so.

Second, not only had the English developed considerable expertise in the business of providing education, they had also learned to take advantage of education in ways that became profoundly important in the colonial setting. They were, after all, increasingly literate, both technically and substantively: more Englishmen knew how to read and more Englishmen actively sought knowledge on a greater variety of subjects, knowledge about what to believe, how to behave, how to raise children, how to stay healthy, how to make money, in effect, how to live and how to die. In addition, the very turbulence of English society during the sixteenth and seventeenth centuries and the uncertainties engendered by that turbulence drove people systematically to search for knowledge and advice that in more stable times they might simply have come by in the informal processes of growing up. Amidst massive religious confusion, people desperately wanted to know what they must do to be saved; amidst massive social confusion, they wanted almost as desperately to know which fork to use and when. The generalization may not have applied to all Englishmen, but it surely applied to a rising proportion of the so-called middling classes, that they came more actively to church, school, books, and experience, as seekers rather than as passive recipients. In short, the educative style of the English underwent a transformation during the Renaissance, and the counterpart of a newly expanded and more complex technology of instruction was a growing number of more aggressive students, utilizing the various opportunities and institutions of education for their own purposes and to their own ends.

Third, the English conception of colonization moved farther and faster than that of any other European power during the early seventeenth century, from an earlier version that saw colonies as exploitative bands of transient men in the employ of metropolitan sponsors to a later version that saw colonies as permanent, self-sustaining communities of men, women, and children. As these communities came into being, they recreated the churches, the schools, the print shops, and especially the family forms they had known in England. The process not only released Anglo-Americans from the vicissitudes of metropolitan interest, emigration, and wherewithal, it also enabled them to propagate their ideas, values, and customs with comparative vigor. The very institutions that ensured self-sufficiency became weapons in the competition of cultures.

Finally, there was the peculiar linking of God, king, and

9

Mammon that stood at the heart of the English notion of empire. The colonists were seen (and indeed they saw themselves) not merely as patriots and adventurers but as agents of God's grand design for the world. It is no surprise to learn that the Puritan preacher John Cotton found scriptural sanction for the voyage to New England in his sermon to the Winthrop fleet at Gravesend in June, 1630: "I will appoint a place for my people Israel, and will plant them, that they may dwell in a place of their own, and move no more; neither shall the children of wickedness afflict them any more, as beforetime." Moreover, as Carl Bridenbaugh has pointed out, Anglican worthies such as Robert Gray and John Donne also quoted Scripture in the cause of colonization. Indeed, any ordinary Englishman seeking his own justification for migrating could find it among the numerous so-called emigration texts sprinkled through Genesis, Joshua, Samuel, Joel, and Matthew. Needless to say, the feeling of being part of God's grand design proved enormously energizing. It suffused colonial politics and commerce with a zealous sense of righteousness, and it bound together the institutions of colonial education with a heady sense of purpose, as the colonists went about the work of creating and sustaining Zion. That such millennial aspirations were utterly utopian seems to have added to their power rather than detracting from it—at least in the beginning. Later on, when reality made itself felt with a vengeance, millennialism reappeared in variant forms, gaining new vigor from the very bleakness of the colonial environment.[3]

[3] Bridenbaugh, *Vexed and Troubled Englishmen*, p. 402. The scriptural passage is from II Sam. 7:10.

II

THE INTERPRETATION I have propounded here is a version of Edward Eggleston's "transit of civilization from England to America," though the transit itself, of course, was a much more complex phenomenon than Eggleston realized. English culture was itself changing and in conflict during the sixteenth and seventeenth centuries, and it was selectively transmitted in any case, so that some ideas and institutions that were fairly prevalent in the metropolis were scarcely evident in the colonies, and vice versa. Moreover, those ideas and institutions that did make their way to America began to undergo subtle changes almost as soon as they arrived, taking on different form and coloration in the new environment. Finally, while there is no denying that the burden of cultural diffusion was westward, the New World did work its influence on the Old, through new products, such as maize, potatoes, persimmons, raspberries, and tobacco, and new ideas, some of which were actually English ideas refracted through the colonial experience.[4]

Education was doubly involved in the transit. It was part and parcel of the process of cultural transmission, affording the colonists access to the political, moral, and technological wisdom of the West; and it was at the same time a critical element in the heritage transmitted. Like other elements of that heritage, it was changing and in conflict, it was selectively

---

[4] Edward Eggleston, *The Transit of Civilization from England to America in the Seventeenth Century* (New York: D. Appleton & Company, 1900).

transmitted, and it began to alter almost as soon as it had been transplanted. Yet, as Eggleston himself remarked, nothing in human history derives *ex nihilo*; and it is to the ideas and institutions of Renaissance England that we must look for the initial paradigms of American education.

Insofar as the colonists transplanted the English village community to America, they transplanted an educational configuration of household, church, and school, each standing in time-honored relation to the others and all mediating the educative influence of didactic literature. The configuration taught, in different combinations for different orders of the society, the values and substance of piety, civility, and learning.

The family was the foremost component of the configuration and carried by far the greatest burden of educational obligation, providing the young with their earliest ideas about the world and how they ought to believe and behave in it, serving as the locus of organized work and preparation for organized work and mediating the nurturance proffered by other educative institutions. In general, the pedagogy of household education was the pedagogy of apprenticeship, that is, a relentless round of imitation, explanation, and trial and error. In addition, a small proportion of households provided systematic tutoring and regular communal devotion. One might come of age in the household of one's birth or be sent to a household managed by kith or kin, but there was no growing up outside a household, at least if one wanted to stay within the law.

The church carried a somewhat lesser burden of immediate educational obligation but at the same time provided a more efficient conduit for extralocal instruction. Whether "indiscriminate" or "gathered," the congregation was essentially an organized group of families who had submitted themselves, voluntarily or involuntarily, to systematic teaching and discipline by an approved clergy (who did the approving, of course, was long a matter of controversy). The teaching ranged from abstruse symbolic and metaphoric interpretations of the meaning of life to the most elementary details of language and belief; the discipline touched every conceivable aspect of diurnal living over the entire life cycle. From stained-glass windows portraying the pious life, to ceremonials symbolizing the meaning of experience, to systematic preaching, catechizing, and chastisement by the clergy, the church instructed, and its curriculum spanned the entire range of human activity.

The school was somewhat more marginal, in the scope of its obligation and the intensity of its influence. Most English youngsters did not go to school at all; those who did went principally to what was euphemistically called a petty school (or dame school), where they studied reading and writing in the mother tongue intermittently for a year or two under an indifferently prepared instructor. A small proportion, made up entirely of boys, might attend a local grammar school, where, if they stayed the course over six or seven years, they might develop considerable facility in Latin, along with a modest knowledge of Greek and Hebrew. Some grammar schools were day schools, others were boarding schools and became surrogate households for the students who attended them. An even smaller proportion of youngsters, from among those who attended grammar school, might go on to an Oxford or Cambridge college or to one of the Inns of Court to study for a learned profession. Both the grammar schools and the institutions of higher education served increasingly as vehicles for social advancement during the later Tudor and early Stuart eras, with the result that they became more and more attractive to the sons of merchant and gentry families and even to an occasional youngster from a yeoman or artisan family.

Finally, there was the institution of printing, which was closely regulated by the Crown, the established church, and the Stationers' Company, and fairly well concentrated in London, Oxford, Cambridge, and the larger provincial towns—at least until the abolition of the Star Chamber and its decrees in 1641. Much early printed matter was didactic and devotional in character, and served purposes essentially congruent with those of the church. But however assiduous the effort to regulate, the volume of unorthodox material increased steadily, ranging from heretical tracts printed by underground presses (or smuggled in from the Continent) to bawdy chapbooks printed by both subversive presses and official presses—when the authorities weren't looking. Access to both printed matter and the interpretations made of printed matter were largely mediated by family, church, and school, and indeed printing in general served to augment the power and effectiveness of extant educative institutions. Yet, with the spread of literacy, printed matter exerted an independent and potentially liberating influence as well, for individuals could come to printed matter on their own or in concert with other individuals outside the confines of formal educative institutions. Whatever else changed, the possibilities for self-education were immeasurably enhanced.

Such was the educational paradigm with which Anglo-

Americans began. And indeed they reproduced it in the New World—after a fashion. The nuclear family, which had prevailed in England on the eve of settlement, was transplanted to America and became the dominant household form. And, as in England too, nuclear households were embedded in networks of kin: sometimes a network migrated simultaneously, as was the case with a number of Puritan families in 1630; sometimes a network stretched over three thousand miles to become a transatlantic community, with individuals and households crossing back and forth from time to time; and sometimes nuclear households created their own networks in the second and third generations, like the modified extended families of eighteenth-century Andover, Massachusetts, described in such rich detail by Philip J. Greven, Jr. The Puritan church was transplanted to New England, and its characteristic "gathered" congregations became the basis of the congregational polity there; the Anglican church was reproduced in the middle and southern colonies. Both petty schools and grammar schools appeared in all the early colonies, sooner in Virginia and Massachusetts Bay, later in Plymouth and Rhode Island; and Harvard College was established in 1636. And the first colonial print shop was established in Cambridge two years after the founding of Harvard. In effect, all the elements in the English configuration of education had been transplanted to the New World by 1638. By 1747, with the chartering of the College of New Jersey, all the elements had appeared in all the English-speaking regions.[5]

Nevertheless, there were crucial changes over time, in the

---

[5] Philip J. Greven, Jr., *Four Generations: Population, Land, and Family in Colonial Andover, Massachusetts* (Ithaca, N.Y.: Cornell University Press, 1970).

institutions themselves and in their relationships with one another and with the society at large. The household, for example, given the nature of the immigration experience, was initially less embedded in a network of nearby kin. Save in those instances where several blood-related households migrated together or during the course of a single generation, the individual household tended to carry its educational burdens in greater isolation than in England. Of course, neighbors would often serve as surrogates for kin; and, as Greven found, kin networks did come into being over two and three generations. But inasmuch as mobility was a pervasive phenomenon of colonial life—even more so than in contemporary England—households more distant from and freer of kin networks remained a significant fact. In addition, given the chronic shortage of labor in the colonies, formal apprenticeship contracts were difficult to enforce: there was little the authorities could do to youngsters or servants who refused to complete their stated terms, especially in light of the failure of the European guild system (with its surveillance of employment) to take root. Informal apprenticeship arrangements were probably just as difficult to enforce; and, despite the passage of blue laws promising stern punishment to "stubborn and rebellious youth," the ready availability of employment and cheap land offered continuing alternatives to acquiescence in parental control. Not everyone recognized the alternatives, and not everyone took advantage of them; but their presence doubtless had a leavening effect on household education. Finally, children became, to borrow a phrase from Margaret Mead, immigrants in time as well as in space, that is, they became the interpreters of change to their elders, and in the process further transformed traditional teaching and learning roles within the household.[6]

The church also changed significantly under altered social circumstances. In New England, the "gathered" congregation prevailed, doubtless strengthening the effectiveness of church teaching among the "saints" who subscribed voluntarily, though not necessarily among the "sinners" who were forced by law to attend. In the middle and southern colonies, Anglicanism prevailed, but the absence of a colonial bishop and the chronic scarcity of ordained clergymen caused a decided deterioration in the quality of church teaching. And, throughout the colonies, the steady erosion of the authority of religious establishments, the increasing presence of competing sects— Quakers, Presbyterians, Baptists, Mennonites, Lutherans, and later Methodists—and the drastic decline in church membership led to the development of a new church pedagogy, namely, evangelicism. Deprived of traditionally assured clienteles, the churches increasingly reached for new members, and in the process their teachers and their teaching were transformed.

The school changed too, though less profoundly than the church. In the absence of well-prepared teachers and sufficient numbers of students, the distinctions between petty schools and grammar schools tended to blur, and what has been called the general school came into being, teaching English or Latin to students, depending on their abilities and

[6] Margaret Mead, *Culture and Commitment: A Study of the Generation Gap* (New York: The Natural History Press, 1970), pp. 56–57.

desires. Furthermore, given the plenitude of cheap land, endowment became an inefficient form of educational support, with the result that tuition fees and taxes had to be substituted and parents and taxpayers thereby gained a voice in school policy making that was less common in England. As for Harvard, it modeled its program on that of Emmanuel College, Cambridge, and its governance on the traditional English pattern of lay trusteeship; but it awarded its degrees without explicit authority from the king, or Parliament, or even the Massachusetts legislature, and it established no formal relationship with any extant university and indeed developed in isolation from the traditional professional faculties. Yet it clearly managed to maintain scholarly standards, as evidenced by the recognition of its degrees at the British and Continental universities. Later, the College of William and Mary was built on a Scottish rather than an English model, while the College of New Jersey was for all intents and purposes a dissenting academy that granted college degrees.[7]

Native printing was initially confined to Massachusetts, though, after the establishment of presses at St. Mary's City and Philadelphia in 1685, it spread rapidly throughout the colonies. The authorities regulated it closely until the Zenger case in 1735 indicated the reluctance of colonial juries to convict printers on charges of "seditious libel"—for which, read "political criticism." But even before 1735 there were shifts in the character of colonial publications, as printers, lacking ex-

---

[7] On Harvard's early governance, I am indebted to Jurgen Herbst, "The First Three American Colleges: Schools of the Reformation," *Perspectives in American History*, 8 (1974): 5–52.

tensive fonts to print the classics—it was cheaper in any case to import them from Europe—concentrated on a more popular literature of sermons, almanacs, schoolbooks, and later newspapers.

However significant these changes in the individual components of the earliest American configurations of education, it is rather on the shifting relationships among the components and the interactions between the configurations themselves and the communities that sustained them that I should like to focus attention. In the New England towns, for example, the various elements of the configuration of household, church, school, college, and printing press were essentially complementary and mutually reinforcing in the knowledge, values, attitudes, and sensibilities they taught. And the knowledge, values, attitudes, and sensibilities they taught were organized into an explicit and well-articulated *paideia*—a vision of life itself as deliberate cultural and ethical aspiration—that we recognize as early American Puritanism. To the extent that the *paideia* was widely shared during the first and second generations, the diurnal life of the community became educative, in that it was explicitly seen as the proper means of forming human beings to live according to God's law.

In the dispersed counties of Virginia, the configurations of education took another form. There, parishes extended over a hundred square miles; formal schools appeared only in the more densely populated regions; there was no local college or university until 1693; and there was no permanent press until 1730. The result was fourfold. First, the household assumed additional burdens; it doubled up or tripled up, so to speak, and took unto itself educative functions performed by other institutions in England and in New England, serving as a community of devotion in the absence of churches and as a center for the teaching of languages, literature, mathematics, and even the professional arts and sciences in the absence of schools and colleges. Second, the lines became blurred between and among other educative institutions. Churches took on the functions of schools just as families took on the functions of churches. Third, given the absence of a local college until the last years of the seventeenth century, Virginia sent more of its young men abroad for schooling, either to Harvard College or to one of the British or Continental universities. And fourth, Virginia remained more dependent upon English printing and publishing for the maintenance of its cultural and educational life. In effect, all the colonies were part of a transatlantic provincial British community with London (and later Edinburgh and Aberdeen) at its hub; and all the colonies imported printed material and sent children abroad for schooling. But Virginia did so even more than New England, with the household as the principal mediator of the process.

In the heterogeneous communities of the middle colonies, and especially in the market towns of New York and Philadelphia, multiple configurations of education became increasingly the rule. The Quakers, for example, did not believe in "mixed" or "indiscriminate" education but rather preferred what they called "guarded" education. In the terms I have been using here, they preferred their own configuration of education, revolving around the Quaker household, the Quaker meetinghouse, and an occasional Quaker school. So did the

Lutherans, who came in growing numbers from the Palatinate during the eighteenth century and who used guarded education to perpetuate a German *paideia*, with the German language at its core. And so also did the Mennonites and Moravians. In fact, the Mennonites and Moravians extended the notion of guardedness to the point of organizing their own communities in isolation from other religious and ethnic groups, in an effort to maintain their traditional patterns of life free of contamination by the presence of alternative modes. All these minorities tended to preserve their relationships with kith and kin in Europe, so that the situation became one of alternative and occasionally competing transatlantic communities. Indeed, the very fact of guardedness in the New World forced some minority communities into greater dependence on relationships with the Old.

Finally, there was the rather different form of guardedness that characterized the education of Indians and blacks. With respect to the Indians, there was the initial experience of having a new and profoundly different civilization set down forcibly—or if not forcibly at least suddenly—beside their own, a civilization explicitly committed to missionary activity and by no means dedicated to harmonious coexistence. Whatever the perception on either side, there was the reality of two coexisting modes of life and two coexisting configurations of education. At the least, there was the possibility of education implicit in the stark alternative: for the members of each community there was the example of the other. In addition, there was mutual education via instruction and example. And, beyond that, there was the linking and blending of educational activities, as, for example, in the case of an Iroquois youngster who might grow up in the characteristic matriarchal *ohwa-chira* of the tribe and then attend a Christian school or an Anglo-American youngster who might grow up in the characteristic patriarchal household of a New England community and then be taken prisoner and taught the ways of the Wampanoog or the Narragansett, or a community of "praying" Indians such as Natick, Massachusetts, in which tribal ways and Anglo-American ways were mixed in some new and emergent combination.

With respect to the blacks, there was the growing fact of slavery and the associated instruments of repression, of which education (including miseducation) was surely one. As with the Indians, the education represented a new and emergent combination, blending the insistent instruction of a dominant white household (and a church proffering a special version of Christianity for blacks) with the quietly transmitted tradition of an African past. As might be expected, the character of the blend depended significantly on the dominant white family and the local white society, the number and organization of blacks immediately involved (isolated males, for example, or families related through kinship), and the number and organization of blacks nearby.

Clearly, there is no simple calculus for measuring the effects of these diverse educational configurations. At the very least, there were profound ironies. Despite the impressive coherence of the typical New England configuration, for example, we know it was far from omnipotent, as the celebrated case of the merchant Robert Keayne in Massachusetts makes clear. The configuration of education in seventeenth-century Massachusetts operated insistently to nurture Puritans; the diurnal life of trade, commerce, and speculation operated no less insistently to nurture Yankees. And, indeed, as Yankee values began to prevail, they were subtly incorporated into the teaching of Yankee households, leading to a dissonance or disjunction in the larger educational configuration during the later seventeenth century. One is reminded of the Yankee traders who prayed on their knees on Sunday and preyed on their neighbors all the rest of the week. In any case, Captain Edward Johnson was already lamenting by the middle of the seventeenth century, "An overeager desire after the world hath so seized on the spirits of many that the chief end of our coming hither is forgotten; and notwithstanding all of the powerful means used, we stand at a stay, as if the Lord had no farther work for his people to do but every bird to feather his own nest." And Cotton Mather put it even more tersely in writing of colonial Plymouth: "Religion brought forth prosperity, and the daughter destroyed the mother." [8]

The story of the Society for the Propagation of the Gospel in Foreign Parts provides another case in point. Founded in England in 1701 to combat atheism, infidelity, and "popish superstition and idolatry" in His Majesty's plantations, colonies, and factories beyond the seas, the Society developed the largest, most systematized, and best-financed program of edu-

---

[8] *Johnson's Wonder-Working Providence, 1638–1651*, edited by J. Franklin Jameson (New York: Charles Scribner's Sons, 1910), p. 260; and Cotton Mather, *Magnalia Christi Americana; or, The Ecclesiastical History of New England*, edited by Thomas Robbins (2 vols.; reprint ed.; Hartford: Silas Andrus and Son, 1853–55), 1:63.

cation in provincial America, establishing and subsidizing churches, schools, and libraries by the score. Its intent, naturally enough, was to guarantee colonial allegiance to the king and the Anglican church. Its effect, ironically, was to extend literacy in the colonies at precisely the time the Revolutionary literature began to circulate. When the Revolutionaries triumphed in 1783, one of the first things they did was expel the Society.

The story of the Pennsylvania Germans provides yet another example. Arriving in considerable numbers after the 1720s, they evoked growing fear and hostility among the founding English Quakers and Anglicans. One manifestation of this fear and hostility was the organization in 1755 of a substantial effort to Anglicize the Germans through a system of charity schools financed by British as well as American money and set up by a German Reformed clergyman named Michael Schlatter. The Pennsylvania Germans, led by the printer Christopher Saur, resisted the program and ultimately defeated it; in fact, the most important outcome of the project was probably in stimulating the Germans to redouble their efforts to perpetuate their own language and culture. Yet, in the end, the Germans were indeed Anglicized, not by charity schools established for that purpose, but rather by their gradual incorporation into the larger American community that was coming into being via participation in provincial politics, trade, and interdenominational activity.

Beyond the ironies that marked the experience of particular organized ventures and particular social groups, there was the inescapable fact that individual Americans came to educational opportunities with their own purposes and their own agenda and moved through the institutions and configurations of education in their own ways. Consider a few familiar examples, none of which ought to be generalized but all of which make the point. We know, for example, that both John Adams (1735–1826) and Thomas Jefferson (1743–1826) progressed through fairly standard provincial configurations of household, church, school, college, and apprenticeship to the law, the principal differences probably lying in the fact that Adams remained in his familial household and attended church and school in Braintree while Jefferson left his familial household to live with his several pastor-schoolmasters. We know that both built and maintained substantial personal libraries and read voraciously for personal edification, and that both used their correspondence throughout their adult lives to reflect upon and learn from experience. But the educational careers of Roger Sherman (1721–1793) and Patrick Henry (1736–1799) were far more typical of the time. Sherman grew up in a shoemaker's household in Newton, Massachusetts, where he attended the usual church services and school classes and also went on to study Latin with the local minister. He learned the shoemaker's trade from his father and practiced it for a time, and then learned surveying, law, and merchandising on his own. Henry grew up in the household of a planter of moderate means in Hanover County, Virginia, studying Latin with his father, attending the sermons of the Reverend Samuel Davies (and indeed studying with Davies for a time), and then learning law by reading "Coke upon Littleton" and the digest of Virginia statutes on his own.

If we look further to the education of Abigail Adams (1744–1818), Martha Jefferson (1748–1782), Sarah Henry (1738–1775), and Elizabeth Sherman (1725–1760), we learn a bit more—though not enough. Abigail Adams was the daughter of a well-to-do Massachusetts minister and received her initial education in manse and church but had no formal schooling. As her grandson Charles Francis Adams later remarked of her, what she learned she picked up as an "eager gatherer" rather than through "systematic instruction." Martha Jefferson was the daughter of a wealthy Virginia lawyer-planter and probably received her early education in household and church, too—we know that she loved music and played the harpsichord and the piano, but there is no hard evidence on where she learned to play them. Sarah Henry was the daughter of a Virginia planter, and Elizabeth Sherman was the daughter of a Stoughton, Massachusetts, farmer. We know little more about them.[9]

If we venture beyond these wives to several eighteenth-century women who achieved distinction in their own right, we learn still more, though again not enough. Jane Colman Turell (1708–1735), for example, was a textbook case of the child prodigy. The daughter of Benjamin Colman, the liberal pastor of Boston's Brattle Street Church, she is reported to have learned her letters before she was two and the greater part of the catechism before she was four, to have composed original hymns before she was twelve, and to have read the entire

[9] *Letters of Mrs. Adams*, edited by Charles Francis Adams (4th ed.; Boston: Wilkins, Carter, and Company, 1848), p. xxiv. See also Janet Whitney, *Abigail Adams* (Boston: Little, Brown and Company, 1947).

collection of English poetry and polite prose in her father's library before she was eighteen—all under the zealous guidance of her parents. She married the young minister Ebenezer Turell in 1726 and went on to write poetry, reflective essays, and even "some pieces of wit and humor," while rearing four children and overseeing the manse in Medford. Alas, she died prematurely, at the age of twenty-seven.[10]

Mercy Otis Warren (1728–1814) is better known. She grew up in Barnstable, Massachusetts, the third child and first daughter of a well-to-do merchant-farmer who also served as judge of the Court of Common Pleas and colonel in the militia. Characteristically, the Otises arranged to have their sons tutored in preparation for Harvard, and characteristically, too—at least it was common among eighteenth-century families whose daughters subsequently achieved distinction—the Otises permitted Mercy to sit in on her brothers' lessons and to browse freely in their tutor's library (the tutor, incidentally, was her uncle, the pastor of Barnstable). Later, after her marriage to an able Harvard alumnus named James Warren, her household in Plymouth became a gathering place for anti-British activists, and she began to write on behalf of the Revolutionary cause—first poems, then satirical plays, and then, following the outbreak of hostilities, a three-volume history of the Revolution itself. As is well known, the history had a pronounced Jeffersonian bias, which irritated the Warrens' friend John Adams, one of those who had encouraged Mercy Warren to write the history in the first place. "History," old Adams

---

[10] Benjamin Colman, *Reliquiae Turellae* (Boston: S. Kneeland & T. Green, 1735), p. 86.

remarked testily to Elbridge Gerry, "is not the province of the ladies." [11]

Now, the difficulty with all this is that the Adamses, the Jeffersons, the Henrys, the Shermans, the Turells, and the Warrens are familiar precisely because they were atypical. What of their several million contemporaries who did not make their way into the *Dictionary of American Biography* or *Notable American Women?* What can we say about their education? Less, I fear, than we should like, and most of that by inference. Most whites came of age in nuclear households more or less in touch with networks of kin, some of them transatlantic. Most were taught via apprenticeship, in their own households or in other households, whatever skills they used in connection with the work they did. Most were probably subjected to some systematic church teaching, though estimates of church membership run at only about a quarter of the population or less. Well under half were likely to have had any formal schooling, and that sporadically and intermittently, though there were some New England towns in which experience with schooling was virtually universal. Most probably learned directly, on occasion, from newspapers, almanacs, and the Bible, gleaning news and other information and acquiring interpretations of the world that helped give meaning and order to events.

Two themes emerge from this discussion: first, the absolute centrality of the household in all childhood education and

[11] John Adams to Elbridge Gerry, April 17, 1813, "Warren-Adams Letters," *Collections of the Massachusetts Historical Society*, 73 (1925): 380. See also Katharine Anthony, *First Lady of the Revolution: The Life of Mercy Otis Warren* (Garden City, N.Y.: Doubleday & Company, 1958).

most later education, particularly that of women, and second, the energizing role of self-education, obviously for men and even more so for women. The themes are salient, of course, in that great classic of early American education, Benjamin Franklin's *Autobiography*. The document can be read on at least three levels, first, as a source for the actualities of provincial education, second, as Franklin's idealized portrayal of the education of a "rising people," and third, as a pivotal influence in the education of the nineteenth- and twentieth-century Americans who later studied it. But however we read the *Autobiography*, as actuality or as idealization, it is in the last analysis the story of an individual making his way through the contemporary configurations of education on both sides of the Atlantic, utilizing education for his own purposes and then going beyond to create new educative institutions, again for his own purposes. And, whatever we learn from it about the eighteenth century, there is no doubt that it transmitted to the nineteenth and twentieth centuries an activist educative style that placed self-education and self-determined education at the core of the American experience. Indeed, the document affected the very way in which Americans would come to write autobiography in the generations ahead, namely, as the larger education of the individual in the active living of American life. [12]

---

[12] *The Autobiography of Benjamin Franklin*, edited by Leonard W. Labaree *et al.* (New Haven: Yale University Press, 1964).

III

THERE REMAINS the problem of the relation of the educational institutions and configurations of provincial America to the character of the larger society and in particular to the movement for independence. What can we suggest with any degree of confidence?

It goes without saying that there was considerable diversity in the nature and character of educational institutions in different provinces and in different parts of the same province, though I would argue on the whole that the institutions and configurations of provincial education became more similar than different during the eighteenth century, despite the substantial German and Scotch-Irish immigrations. The churches reached out for new clienteles during the awakenings, dramatically changing their pedagogical styles and in the process creating their own configurations of associated families, youth groups, and study centers. The actual number of churches rose during the eighteenth century, as did the number of different sects and denominations represented by the churches, but it is questionable whether the churches kept pace with the growth of population. The schools, on the other hand, increased steadily, not only in absolute number, but also in proportion to the population, and they began to diversify as well, particularly in the larger towns and cities. There were literally thousands of them, teaching every manner of subject, art, and skill—in rented rooms, churches, meetinghouses, and abandoned huts as well as in buildings specifically called schoolhouses. In addition, there were scores of academies, many of them offering college-level instruction, and with the founding of Dartmouth in 1769 there were nine chartered colleges. Finally, there were some forty presses scattered through the provinces—after James Johnston transferred his print shop from Great Britain to Savannah in 1762, every province had at least one—and they issued an increasing flow of books, pamphlets, almanacs, and newspapers. All things considered, I think it fair to suggest that the popularization of American education was already well under way by the time of the Revolution. More people and more diverse groups of people had access to more institutions and more diverse institutions subject to more popular and more diversely popular control. This is not to suggest that the hoi polloi had taken over Harvard, or Trinity Church in New York, or even James Johnston's press in Georgia; it is merely to suggest that a discernible change was taking place in a discernible direction.

What, then, were the effects of this education on provincial society? The problem is extraordinarily complex, and requires disentangling the outcomes of education from the more general march of events. One begins, I suspect, with literacy, as a fundamental index of cultural vitality. In my own analyses of this phenomenon, I have attempted to go beyond traditional definitions of literacy as the mere technical ability to read a passage or write one's name and to conceive of literacy instead as an interaction between an individual with a measure of technical ability and a particular literary environment. And, following that conception, I have sought to distinguish between what I would call inert literacy, in which a minimum technical ability is combined with limited motivation, need, and opportunity (the literacy of the sixteenth-century yeoman who learned to read the Christian liturgy and nothing else would be an excellent illustration), and a more liberating literacy, in which a growing technical ability is combined with expanding motivation, need, and opportunity (the literacy of the American colonists following the Stamp Act crisis of the 1760s is a useful case in point).

With this broader definition in mind, I would venture three assertions about literacy in colonial America. First, largely (and I must confess reluctantly) on the basis of traditional signature counts, I would contend that literacy rates among transplanted Europeans of the first and second generations remained roughly comparable to those in the European metropolis; and I would stress by way of explanation the crucial role of familial and church instruction in colonial regions where schools were not widely available. Second, using statistics of newspaper circulation, which I would judge a more dependable measure of literacy than signature counts, I would argue that the character of American literacy changed fundamentally in the eighteenth century, from inert literacy to liberating literacy—in essence, a growing number of readers (who had learned to read in households, churches, schools, and via self-instruction) stimulated an expanding press, which in turn stimulated the motivation to read. Third, comparing the American colonies first with the English metropolis and then with Ireland (which was colonized by the English at roughly the same time as North America), I would maintain that literacy rates in the colonies on the eve of the Revolution were only slightly below those in England (rates among whites were roughly the same as those in provincial England, but extensive illiteracy among American blacks and Indians lowered the overall American rates) and significantly above those in Ireland, testifying to the vitality and efficacy of American educational institutions. [13]

Now, the mere fact of what I have referred to as liberating literacy implies a number of related phenomena. First, access to printed materials—particularly those emanating from a variety of sources in a relatively permissive atmosphere—in its very nature opens a person's mind to change, to new ideas and influences, to new goals and aspirations. An endless vista of choices and discoveries is laid before the newly literate that we who have been accustomed to universal literacy over many generations are wont to underplay. Whatever else freedom means, it does mean genuine choice, the awareness of real alternatives that can be acted upon. Of course, literacy can scarcely confer agency, in and of itself; but literacy does hold the makings of agency insofar as it helps people to see beyond the boundaries of household, parish, and neighborhood. Second, literacy simultaneously systematizes and individualizes experience. It makes possible new technologies of organization, symbolized best, perhaps, by merchant's accounts or the Book of Common Prayer, at the same time as it facilitates the self-conscious individualization of belief and behavior—consider, alternatively, the private handwritten letter or *The Pilgrim's Progress*, with its image of Christian holding his book

---

[13] I reviewed my theses concerning literacy in the context of the recent literature in "Reading, Writing, and Literacy," *The Review of Education*, 1 (1975): 517–521.

and asking, "What shall I do?" To the extent that literacy rationalizes experience, it can and often does strengthen the power of extant educative institutions; to the extent that literacy individualizes experience, it can and does become a tool for reflecting upon extant educative institutions and criticizing their efforts. Third, literacy in an expanding literary environment seems to create a demand for more literacy, both within the same generation and into the next: the newly literate want more literacy for themselves, for their contemporaries, and for their children. Such was certainly the case in provincial America.[14]

All these phenomena, of course, are related to the larger process we call modernization, and there has been a good deal of controversy in recent years concerning precisely how and when that process went forward in early America. Daniel Boorstin has portrayed it as beginning in the seventeenth century and continuing throughout the eighteenth. Richard D. Brown has portrayed it as beginning in the seventeenth century, suffering a degree of retardation and even reversal in the eighteenth, and then reviving during the era of independence. And Kenneth A. Lockridge has portrayed it as beginning during the early decades of the nineteenth century. My own position is that modernization began in the seventeenth century—it was a prominent feature of the civilization in motion that was transplanted—and that it continued into the eighteenth. But it was neither a linear development nor the sole process at

[14] In discussing the consequences of literacy, I have drawn upon David Riesman, *The Oral Tradition, the Written Word, and the Screen Image* (Yellow Springs, Ohio: The Antioch Press, 1956) and Jack Goody and Ian Watt, "The Consequences of Literacy," *Comparative Studies in History and Society*, 5 (1962–63): 304–345.

work in provincial society. Indeed, the very precariousness and relative rootlessness of colonial life led to a contrapuntal traditionalism, in which elites sought to reproduce the more traditional elements of metropolitan life. Yet, whatever conclusion one reaches on the matter, two assertions must be made concerning the relationship between literacy and modernization. First, the effects of literacy are inescapably complex and often conflicting, contributing simultaneously to liberation and constraint, with the ultimate balance between the two depending largely on social circumstances. And second, whatever the effects of literacy per se, they must always be assessed within a more comprehensive context of political, economic, and social events. Put otherwise, reading can be liberating or constraining in its effects; and, even when it is on balance liberating, the sense of possibility it engenders can be confirmed or denied by individual experience and the march of events. Whether the slave loves or hates his chains often has little to do with whether he is forced to wear them. Yet slavemasters were sufficiently concerned with the effects of literacy to enact legislation making it unlawful to teach slaves to read. [15]

The consequences of the increase in the number of schools—in proportion to the population and in relation to the other components of the provincial configuration of education—were equally complex. In the first place, there were

[15] Daniel J. Boorstin, *The Americans: The Colonial Experience* (New York: Random House, 1958); Richard D. Brown, "Modernization and the Modern Personality in Early America, 1600–1865: A Sketch of a Synthesis," *The Journal of Interdisciplinary History*, 2 (1971–72): 201–228; and Kenneth A. Lockridge, *Literacy in Colonial New England: An Enquiry into the Social Context of Literacy in the Early Modern West* (New York: W. W. Norton & Company, 1974).

many different kinds of schools, from the public town schools of New England to the private entrepreneurial schools of New York and Philadelphia to the so-called old-field schools of Virginia, which were for all intents and purposes private tutors shared by several plantation households. In the second place, there was virtually no systematization of schooling in the modern sense; as Carl F. Kaestle has pointed out, the term "system" in eighteenth-century education referred to a curriculum or a method or especially a sequence for teaching a subject (thus a system of reading or a system of arithmetic) and not to a bureaucratic organization. The experience of schooling was really quite individualized, with youngsters in any schoolroom tending to work seriatim with the teacher. The very range of ages represented in most schools ultimately necessitated such a procedure. And, in the third place, schooling slowly became more secular during the eighteenth century, not wholly secular but more secular, as witness the differences between successive eighteenth-century editions of *The New England Primer*, or between the *Primer* and the textbooks by Thomas Dilworth, which came into fashion after 1750.[16]

Even more fundamental, perhaps, is the generic polarity inherent in schooling. On the one hand, schooling, like every other agency of deliberate nurture, socializes: it tends to convey the prevailing values and attitudes of the community or subcommunity that sponsors it. On the other hand, schooling, insofar as it exposes individuals to people and ideas not already encountered at home or in church, liberates and extends. As

[16] Carl F. Kaestle, *The Evolution of an Urban School System: New York City, 1750–1850* (Cambridge, Mass.: Harvard University Press, 1973), p. 161.

with the printed matter that is the essence of its instruction, schooling opens the mind to new options and new possibilities. Hence, the outcomes of schooling are almost invariably contradictory. Schooling—like education in general—never liberates without at the same time limiting. It never empowers without at the same time constraining. It never frees without at the same time socializing. The question is not whether one or the other is occurring in isolation but what the balance is, and to what end, and in light of what alternatives.

Bearing in mind these strictures, I tend to view the growing availability of schooling in provincial America as on balance liberating, seeing in schooling an extension of possibility for anyone who managed to venture beyond the confines of home and church. Of course, there is no denying that provincial schools socialized—all schools socialize. But I would insist that on balance schools were more liberating than not for those who attended, especially when one imagines what eighteenth-century America might have been like without schools or what it was, in fact, where there were no schools. Moreover, my argument does not ignore the fact that there was a significant "underclass" of whites, blacks, and Indians in provincial America with little or no access to literacy, or to schooling, or to life alternatives—real or imaginary.

Finally, there is the relation of the configurations of provincial education to the movement for independence, and here the influence was explicit and direct. The Revolution didn't just happen; it was deliberately instigated and fomented by an able group of men and women, who used all the extant agencies of education for their purposes—and even invented some new ones, such as the Committees of Correspondence and the Sons of Liberty. Preachers used the pulpit to sermonize on the God-given liberties and privileges of freeborn men. Teachers used the lectern to nurture ideas of independency, while students organized symbolic actions ranging from burnings in effigy to boycotts of tea—recall that one Tory alumnus of the Yale class of 1750 was moved to characterize his alma mater under Ezra Stiles as "a nursery of sedition, of faction and republicanism." And printers, roused to concerted action by the Stamp Act, taught relentlessly through handbills, broadsides, pamphlets, and especially newspapers—leading David Ramsay later to celebrate their role in his eyewitness history of the Revolution with the observation that in the establishment of independence "the pen and the press had a merit equal to that of the sword." We need only recall that Thomas Paine's *Common Sense* (1776) sold a hundred thousand copies within three months of its appearance and possibly as many as a half-million in all. That means a fifth of the colonial population bought it and a half or more probably read it or heard it read aloud.[17]

In the end, as John Adams aptly put it, the real revolution had been effected before the war had ever begun—"in the minds and hearts of the people." The real revolution had been essentially a matter of popular education.[18]

[17] Thomas Jones, *History of New York During the Revolutionary War*, edited by Edward Floyd De Lancey (2 vols.; New York: Printed for the New York Historical Society, 1879), 1:3; and David Ramsay, *The History of the American Revolution* (2 vols.; Philadelphia: R. Aiken & Son, 1789), 2:319.

[18] John Adams to Hezekiah Niles, February 13, 1818, *The Works of John Adams*, edited by Charles Francis Adams (10 vols.; Boston: Charles C. Little and James Brown, 1851), 10:282.

THE NATIONAL
EXPERIENCE:
1783–1876

THE REVOLUTION was a pivotal event in American history. It was at the same time a reservoir, summing up and gathering together the antecedent past, and a watershed, initiating and directing the flow of the future. And what is fascinating is the extent to which contemporaries on both sides of the Atlantic recognized its auspiciousness. "I think it one of the most important revolutions that has ever taken place in the world," the English Nonconformist Richard Price wrote to Benjamin Rush in the summer of 1783. "It makes a new opening in human affairs which may prove an introduction to times of more light and liberty and virtue than have yet been known." So far as Price was concerned, the Revolution had begun a new era in the history of mankind: it had created a republic more liberal and equitable than had hitherto been known; it had provided a place of refuge for oppressed peoples everywhere; and it had laid the foundations of an empire wherein liberty, science, and virtue would flourish. Next to the introduction of Christianity itself, Price judged, the Revolution had been the single most salutary event in the history of humankind. Rush himself was somewhat more restrained, though no less enthusiastic. "We have changed our forms of government," he later remarked to Price, "but it remains yet to effect a revolution in our principles, opinions, and manners, so as to accommodate them to the forms of government we have adopted. This is the most difficult part of the business of the patriots and legislators of our country." [1]

It was to this revolution in the principles, opinions, and manners of the people that Rush and his generation turned during the decades following the War of Independence. Politically, the Republic was defined in the various state and national constitutions and in the debates that surrounded their ratification; and, though there was endless controversy over particular issues, there was considerable agreement on such "self-evident truths" as the sovereignty of the people, the separation of powers, mixed government, and representation. Along with these, and inextricably intertwined with them, there was widespread acknowledgment of the crucial significance of education. Insisting with Montesquieu that the principles of education be relative to the forms of government, Americans maintained that while monarchies needed an edu-

[1] Richard Price to Benjamin Rush, June 26, 1783, Rush Manuscripts, Library Company of Philadelphia; and Benjamin Rush to Richard Price, May 25, 1786, *Letters of Benjamin Rush*, edited by L. H. Butterfield (2 vols.; Princeton, N.J.: Princeton University Press, 1951), 1:388.

cation to status that would fix each class of the citizenry to its proper place in the social order, republics needed an education to virtue that would motivate all men to choose public over private interest. By virtue, of course, Americans in the 1780s and 1790s implied some proper combination of piety, civility, and learning, with the definitions ranging from Thomas Paine's rationalistic humanitarianism to Timothy Dwight's Puritan orthodoxy. And by education they meant the full panoply of institutions that played a part in shaping human character—families and churches, schools and colleges, public newspapers, voluntary associations, and, most important perhaps in an era of constitution making, the laws. Yet they saw no simple relationship between people and politics, recognizing on the one hand that republics could not thrive in the absence of widespread public virtue and on the other hand that no system of government could in the last analysis stake its existence on the assumption of such public virtue. So, being above all practical, they proceeded on two fronts, establishing educational arrangements that would nurture piety, civility, and learning in the populace at large and erecting a political system through which the inevitable conflicts of crass self-interest might be resolved.

Beyond this, they argued for a truly American education, purged of all vestiges of older monarchical forms and designed to create a cohesive and independent citizenry. Deploring the widespread mimicry of European ways, they urged the deliberate fashioning of a new republican character, rooted in the American soil, based on an American language and literature, steeped in American art, history, and law, and committed to

43

the promise of an American culture. In part, this implied a conscious rejection of Europe, a turning away from what was widely perceived as a thousand-year tradition of feudalism, despotism, and corruption. But, more important, it implied a conscious act of creation; for the American character had yet to be defined, and on its proper definition rested the health and safety of the new nation.

In short, the Revolution confirmed and initiated in education, as it did in politics. It gathered together developments tending toward the popularization of education that had been in the making for at least a generation, and it invested them with revived millennial purpose. New groups of immigrants came in unprecedented numbers, bringing time-honored ideas and institutions from Europe, Africa, and Asia—the Irish brought a particular form of the Roman Catholic church; the Angolese brought a particular form of the matriarchal family; and the Chinese brought a particular form of the mutual benefit society. Native-born Americans, in turn, reached out to other countries for ideas and institutions that seemed to promise educational advance—to England for the Sunday school and the lyceum, to Switzerland for methods of child rearing, to France for models of military training. And autochthonous institutions came into being as the deliberate fruits of human invention—one thinks of Charles Willson Peale's museum, James Gordon Bennett's penny newspaper, Jonathan Baldwin Turner's agricultural college, and Joseph Smith's Mormon family. In the process, there flowered during the first century of national life an authentic vernacular in education, which stands in retrospect—granting its flaws, its imperfections, and even its several tragic shortcomings—as among the half-dozen most interesting aspects of nineteenth-century American civilization.

II

THE INSTITUTIONS of American education changed significantly during the first century of nationhood, partly by way of response to more general developments in Western civilization and partly as a result of uniquely American conditions. The household underwent the first phases of the transformation scholars have generally associated with the phenomenon of modernization, though that transformation occurred variously in different regions and among different ethnic, religious, and racial groups. The great Irish migration of the 1840s and 1850s, for example, brought the Irish stem family to the cities of the Northeast, with its characteristic parent and child roles and its intimate relationships with a particular version of the Roman Catholic church. Similarly, the great Chinese migration of the 1860s and 1870s brought the Chinese joint family to the cities of the Far West, with its network of kin extending five thousand miles across the Pacific and its intimate relationship with the largely alien institutions of Buddhism and Confucianism. And the Mormons created their special version of the polygamous family, once again in intimate relationship with a special version of a Hebraic-Christian church. All these familial systems were profoundly affected by modernization in the nineteenth century, but in profoundly different ways.

Yet, that fact notwithstanding, there were certain more general trends that can be discerned. Most important, perhaps, was the shift of various kinds of work from the household to the factory, the shop, and the market—a shift that dramatically altered the character of apprenticeship and the educative roles of parents vis-à-vis those of other adults. The shift occurred first in the cities and factory towns of the East, but it augured changes that were to become increasingly widespread over time. Of a different order, perhaps, though significant in that it served as a countervailing influence to those set in motion by the relocation of work, was the development of the idea of domesticity. Taught insistently to an emerging middle class by every manner of treatise, self-instruction manual, and women's magazine, the idea of domesticity sharpened the boundaries between household and community and rendered them more impenetrable, designating more stringently than before who had the right and responsibility to teach (the mother beyond all others, and then the father, grandparents, uncles, and aunts) and who needed to be counteracted (a broadly undefined "them," including employers, self-interested corrupters of youth, and strangers in general). Finally, there was the effect of what George W. Pierson has called the "M-factor" in American history—the business of incessant geographic movement—on the relationship of household and kin. We know that in the settlement of new regions kinship ties often determined who actually came, especially in the second and third waves. But we also know that, as early as the census of 1850, roughly a quarter of the native population was living in states other than those in which they were born. To the extent that the American household was embedded in a network of kin, those kin were geographically distant rather than close by.[2]

Paralleling the contrapuntal influences acting upon the household itself was the proliferation of special institutions to assume functions formerly carried on by the household, namely, the almshouse, the asylum, the reformatory, and the penitentiary. All were organized as custodial institutions, and all, with the possible exception of the almshouse, professed rehabilitative, or educative, aspirations, though the tension between such aspirations and the realities of custodianship was manifest from the beginning. Their development, I suspect, stemmed as much from the demographic conditions of nineteenth-century America as from the more peculiarly Jacksonian ambience that David J. Rothman has described as central to their emergence, and indeed they all had precedents in England and on the Continent—not a one arose *ex nihilo*. But what is significant about these new institutions is the extent to which they were explicitly seen, on the one hand, as surrogates for families and schools—the metaphors of household and schooling abound in the literature of custodial institutions—and, on the other hand, as complements to families and schools in the building and maintenance of the virtuous society.[3]

Institution building, of course, is a common element in modernization; and, quite beyond the proliferation of quasi-familial agencies, the nineteenth century witnessed the cre-

[2] George W. Pierson, "The M-Factor in American History," *American Quarterly*, 14 (1962): 275–289, and *The Moving American* (New York: Alfred A. Knopf, 1973).

[3] David J. Rothman, *The Discovery of the Asylum: Social Order and Disorder in the New Republic* (Boston: Little, Brown and Company, 1971).

ation and development of a plethora of new educational forms. The lyceum, for example, was imported from England during the 1820s and flourished during the quarter-century before the Civil War. The museum, the botanical garden, the agricultural fair, and the circus came into their own and were used variously in the service of science, art, and entrepreneurship—though whatever else they were intended to accomplish, they almost always educated. Learned academies sprang up on the Franklin model; professional societies and craft unions came into being, with pretensions to improving the quality of production and service; and publishers like the brothers Harper created mail-order series, libraries, and how-to-do-it magazines of every sort and variety. Whatever else may have marked the age, it was decidedly a time of multitudinousness in education.

The churches continued to be shaped by the forces of evangelicism, and in the process they too created new institutions of deliberate nurture. I myself have had more difficulty than some in distinguishing between a first and a second awakening; but, however one solves that historiographical problem, there is no denying that the revivalism that emanated from Yale under Timothy Dwight early linked with the revivalism that emanated from Cane Ridge under Barton W. Stone, and that the two in combination sparked the great organizing movement led by the Methodists and Baptists in the South and by the "Presbygational" interdenominational agencies in the North and West. The outcome was a vast educational campaign to save the West from sin in general and Roman Catholicism in particular. Needless to say, the entire effort was essentially educational. In the first place, what is referred to in religious history as Methodist "discipline" was really an organizational device to teach certain general outlooks and behaviors to the laity—recall that the English word "discipline" derives from the Latin word *disciplina*, which means "instruction." Second, the churches saw themselves in a traditional role as energizers of other educative institutions: they created new agencies like the camp meeting and the Sunday school to propagate their ideas, and they sought to inspirit more traditional agencies like the family, the school, the college, the press, and the voluntary association. Indeed, I have tended to view the 1830s and 1840s as an era of massive effort to respiritualize the institutions of nurture, and insofar as that effort was successful, agencies such as schools and colleges continued to teach the ideals of the revival long after the revival itself had lost its momentum. Finally, in their attempt to create a new republican individual of virtuous character, abiding patriotism, and prudent wisdom, the churches developed an American *paideia* that was for all intents and purposes a Protestant *paideia*. Indeed, they did everything in their power to render the two indistinguishable and therefore interchangeable.

Actually, if citizens turned to the churches as instruments for the development of a new republican character, it was because the churches, formally disestablished after 1833, volunteered insistently for the task and were persuasive. If citizens turned also to the schools, it was because a group of able publicists convinced them that the schools were the most appropriate public educators of the emerging republican polity. Recall that the number of schools, both in absolute terms and in proportion to the population, had begun to increase significantly during the eighteenth century throughout the provinces. That increase persisted into the nineteenth century, to the point where schooling had become widely available in the older, more settled areas by the 1820s and 1830s. But the diversity of schooling also persisted, so that what was available came in many models, from the charity schools of New York and Philadelphia, to the town-sponsored ventures of New England, to the various church-supported systems maintained by the Quakers, the Presbyterians, and the Episcopalians, to the quasi-public academies that sprang up in every region of the country. The primary accomplishment of the public-school movement of the 1840s and 1850s was obviously not to initiate popular schooling. What the movement actually did achieve was, first, to extend schooling to those regions, particularly in the West, where it was still sparse; second, to regularize schooling in those regions where it was still intermittent; and third, to systematize schooling in those regions where it was already prevalent. As is often the case with reform movements, what occurred was a diffusion and a consolidation, but not a beginning. Yet, the fact that schooling became public in a *de jure* sense at precisely the time that churches remained public solely in a *de facto* sense had prodigious consequences for the future; for localities and states found a political leverage with respect to the schools that they no longer enjoyed with respect to the churches. The result was that the schools became the public's agencies for creating and re-creating publics. Whereas schools and churches were commingled in the public mind of the 1830s and 1840s, they were more separate and separable in the public mind of the 1860s and 1870s.

The school performed many functions: it provided young-sters with an opportunity to become literate in a standard American English via the Webster speller and the McGuffey readers; it offered youngsters a common belief system combin-ing undenominational Protestantism and nonpartisan patrio-tism; it afforded youngsters an elementary familiarity with sim-ple arithmetic, bits and pieces of literature, history, geography, and some rules of life at the level of the maxim and proverb; it introduced youngsters to an organized subsociety other than the household and church that observed such norms as punctuality, achievement, competitiveness, fair play, merit, and respect for adult authority; and it laid before youngsters processes of reasoning, argument, and criticism— indeed, processes of learning to learn—that were more or less different from thought processes proffered earlier and else-where. None of this is to argue that youngsters necessarily learned these things or learned them in the same way, for then as now children came to school with their own tempera-ments, their own histories, and their own agenda, having been educated by other institutions before entering school and con-tinuing to be educated by other institutions while attending school.

Whatever was learned and however well, the school, in concert with the church, prepared youngsters for several kinds of adult experience. It eased their way into productive work outside the household, where literacy and punctuality, adher-ence to rules and procedures, and the ability to cooperate with people of varying ages who were not kin would be expected. It made possible various uses, and misuses, of printed material, from its uncritical consumption as propaganda to its intelligent employment as an instrument of deliberate self-instruction. And it taught the skills needed for participation in the voluntary associations that sprang up in such large numbers during the early nineteenth century as vehicles for everything from mutual consciousness-raising to systematic political lobbying. Indeed, the American polity during the nineteenth century may actually be conceived as a welter of competing voluntary organizations, each using print for its own propagandistic purposes. In the collision of ideas and programs lay an education for Americans, not necessarily at the high and cultivated level foreseen by Jefferson, but at a fruitful popular level nonetheless. Not everyone recognized the alternatives or was able to take advantage of them, but the cacophony that was nineteenth-century America did proffer a growing number of options to a growing number of people and groups.

The celebration of alternatives here should be joined to an obvious caveat about people who had no alternatives at all or fewer alternatives than most. There were the slaves, locked into a closed authority system that shaped them within its confines far more decisively than any combination of church, school, print, and voluntary association, though a recently completed dissertation by Thomas Lane Webber furnishes ample evidence that the slaves on larger plantations did develop their own educative institutions, centered in the families, the clandestine congregations, and the storytellers of the so-called quarter-community, institutions that were immensely effective in transmitting notions of black pride, human dignity, and the possibility of freedom from one generation of blacks to another. There were the Indians, increasingly locked into a variant of the closed authority system called the reservation, with its contradictory combination of tribal and missionary or governmental institutions. There were the numerous groups of religious and ethnic pariahs, who were involuntarily kept from the mainstream of the society, like the Mormons, or who voluntarily withdrew, like the Mennonites. And finally there were the separate worlds of the two sexes, which remained differentially circumscribed with respect to life options in general and educational options in particular.[4]

Beyond the common schools and academies, there were the colleges, universities, and other so-called seminaries of learning. Such institutions were founded in droves during the first century of the Republic, and there is really no way of counting them accurately, partly because of the looseness of definition and partly because they were not only founded in large numbers but they expired in large numbers too. Emerson Davis counted a hundred twenty colleges in 1851, along with forty-two theological seminaries, thirty-seven medical schools, and a dozen law schools; and he had fairly stringent canons of classification—there must have been many more. By 1875, there were some seven hundred colleges and universities, over a hundred theological seminaries, some three dozen law

---

[4] Thomas Lane Webber, "The Education of the Slave Quarter Community: White Teaching and Black Learning on the Ante-Bellum Plantation" (unpublished doctoral thesis, Teachers College, Columbia University, 1975). For the contradictory configurations of Indian education, see Robert F. Berkhofer, Jr., *Salvation and the Savage: An Analysis of Protestant Missions and American Indian Response, 1787–1862* (Lexington: University of Kentucky Press, 1965). For networks of women as sexually segregated educative institutions, see Carroll Smith-Rosenberg, "The Female World of Love and Ritual: Relations Between Women in Nineteenth-Century America," *Signs: Journal of Women in Culture and Society*, 1 (1975): 1–29.

schools, and almost eighty medical and dental schools—and recall, these were the ones that survived. Many of these institutions remained loosely defined for years: the theological schools taught general as well as professional subjects, and the medical and dental schools taught popular science. The colleges are especially interesting, having come into being for every conceivable purpose, including community boosterism plain and simple. The military academy at West Point was established in 1802 to train officers for the armed services, and ended up also training most of the pre–Civil War engineers in the United States who did not come solely via the route of apprenticeship. The College of the City of New York was created in 1847 to train New York City youngsters who could not afford to pay for higher education; Michigan Agricultural College was founded in 1855 to train farmers; Vassar College was founded in 1861 to train women; and Howard University was founded in 1867 to train blacks. Out of all this came the patchwork quilt of American higher education. Yet the quilt was pastel rather than deep-hued, for almost as soon as one of these institutions was founded, its clientele began to diversify and demand comprehensiveness. The phenomenon, I believe, can be summed up in three generalizations: (1) groups that could not obtain what they wanted from extant institutions of higher learning founded new institutions for special purposes or special clienteles; (2) virtually as soon as the new institutions were founded, they began to broaden their purposes, owing most often to the diversification of their clienteles; and (3) despite this broadening of purpose, the institutions continued to bear upon themselves the enduring marks of their origins. Michigan Agricultural College has evolved into a multipurpose institution that trains comparatively few farmers; Vassar College is coeducational; and Howard University is multiracial. But all three institutions have special flavors and qualities that derive in part from their special origins.[5]

One could go on about the individual institutions of education, but once again I would prefer to dwell upon the configurations of the era. What can be said about the way in which the several institutions, each changing over time in interaction with the society at large, patterned themselves? I would venture four generalizations. First, the basic configuration of American education during the period remained one of household, church, school, college, and publisher; but at least three significant components were added: institutions of organized work external to the household, principally the factory but also the mine, the shop, the office, the retail establishment, and the government bureau; custodial institutions with the explicit purpose of rehabilitating their clients; and additional institutions for the diffusion of special kinds of knowledge, such as museums, lyceums, and botanical gardens. Second, there was a shift in the relative power of the several components of the educational configuration, partly because there were more of them and partly because the society shifted the foci of its economic and spiritual investments. Thus, I would maintain that the educative influence of the school and the newspaper grew in relation to that of the household and

---

[5] Emerson Davis, *The Half Century; or, A History of Changes That Have Taken Place, and Events That Have Transpired, Chiefly in the United States, Between 1800 and 1850* (Boston: Tappan and Whittemore, 1851), pp. 75–83.

the church, and that the educative influence of the external place of work increasingly mediated the influence of all other education during the years of active adult employment—it simply loomed larger as a selective shaper of aspiration, taste, and outlook, though obviously in interaction with household and church. That said, a third generalization must immediately be juxtaposed, namely, that there was the continuously revitalized influence of the evangelical church working in concert with households, Sunday schools, common schools, colleges, Bible and tract societies, missionary organizations, and specialized publishing houses. The relationships among these agencies were political, pedagogical, and personal: they were controlled, supported, and managed by the same kinds and classes of people; they used methods and materials reflecting a common subscription to evangelical values and an evangelical exhortative style; and they embraced the same sorts of people, teachers as well as learners. Finally, a fourth generalization must be added, namely, the repeated caveat that the slave plantation, the Indian reservation, and the voluntary and involuntary ghettos created by utopian striving and systematic segregation all persisted, as alternative educational configurations more or less isolated from the mainstream.

Like the generalizations regarding the colonial era, however, the generalizations regarding the nineteenth century apply variously in different communities. Let us consider, by way of example, Lowell, Massachusetts; Sumter District, South Carolina; and Macoupin County, Illinois. The reasons for the choices are fairly obvious. Lowell offers insight into the impact of the factory, though it is important to recall that the so-called Waltham system of cotton manufacture that prevailed there represented only one among several patterns of early industrial development. Sumter District provides instances of large plantations with substantial black quarter-communities comprising a hundred or more slaves, though it is well to bear in mind that such plantations were the exception rather than the rule, not only in Sumter but throughout the pre–Civil War South. And Macoupin County reveals the dynamics of community building on the frontier, though, once again, I am well aware that to have chosen a county in the Texas cattle country or on the Minnesota iron range would have yielded different data.

Lowell originated as part of the town of Chelmsford, situated at the confluence of the Merrimac and Concord rivers in northeastern Massachusetts, some twenty-five miles from Boston. In 1820, it had a population of seven hundred; when it was incorporated as a town in 1826, the population had grown to twenty-five hundred; by the time it was incorporated as a city in 1836, it had grown to eighteen thousand; and, by 1846, it stood at thirty thousand. There had been earlier manufacturing of cloth, bootstraps, glass, and gunpowder, but the transition came in 1825, when the Waltham system of cotton manufacture came to Lowell. The Waltham system involved three central elements: first, corporate ownership; second, the combining of yarn and cloth production under a single roof; and third, the recruitment as workers of young, unmarried women from the surrounding rural region, who lived in company-owned boardinghouses under quasi-familial supervision by company overseers.[6]

[6] The chief secondary works on Lowell are Henry A. Miles, *Lowell, As It Was, and As It Is* (Lowell, Mass.: Powers and Bagley, 1845), Frederick W. Coburn, *History*

Now, there is no denying that Lowell was from the beginning a factory town, a "city of spindles." But to talk exclusively of its factories, as so much of the traditional literature has done, is to offer a one-dimensional view at best. For one thing, Lowell inherited New England's well-established respect and provision for formal schooling. For another, it inherited New England's characteristic concern for social mobility via self-improvement and self-instruction. Third, Lowell was a burgeoning city, and, particularly with the Irish immigration of the 1830s and 1840s, it began to develop new modes of social control for its increasingly heterogeneous population. Finally, Lowell was indeed a factory town, requiring a disciplined work force to satisfy its industrial needs. Now, to ignore the educative agencies other than the factories and their attached dormitories is to risk egregious distortion, since one cannot simply assume that the factory-owners diabolically controlled the entire educative apparatus of the community. The household remained significant; and, since many of the operatives came from communities outside Lowell, the household was an individualizing influence, though selective recruitment did reduce the range of variation. The church remained significant, too, and by 1845 the city boasted

---

of Lowell and Its People (3 vols.; New York: Lewis Historical Publishing Company, 1920), John P. Coolidge, *Mill and Mansion: A Study of Architecture and Society in Lowell, Massachusetts, 1820–1865* (New York: Columbia University Press, 1942), Thomas Bender, *Toward an Urban Vision: Ideas and Institutions in Nineteenth-Century America* (Lexington: University Press of Kentucky, 1975), and Robert F. Dalzell, Jr., "The Rise of the Waltham-Lowell System and Some Thoughts on the Political Economy of Modernization in Ante-Bellum Massachusetts," *Perspectives in American History*, 9 (1975): 227–268. The statistics are drawn from the federal census and the remarkably detailed reports of the Lowell School Committee.

twenty-three separate churches housed in nineteen buildings, representing Congregationalist, Baptist, Universalist, Methodist, Christian, Roman Catholic, Episcopalian, and Unitarian affiliations. It would be foolish to argue that there was collusion or even continuing collaboration among the several churches. Far from it: there was incessant street fighting between Catholics and Protestants even before the extensive influx of Irish in the 1840s, and Harriet Robinson was actually banished from the Congregational church for flirting with Universalist ideas.[7]

The development of Lowell's public schools was impressive. By 1840 the city had built what must have been one of the most complete systems of public schooling of any community its size; by 1850 there were forty-six primary schools, thirteen grammar schools, and a high school, and of 5,432 children between the ages of four and sixteen, there was an average daily attendance of 4,347. What is more, there is every evidence that the board of education and the superintendent were fairly diligent about enforcing laws mandating a minimum period of schooling for children under fifteen who wanted to work in the mills. There was also a significant attendance at the Irish grammar schools, bespeaking the willingness of Irish parents to use the schools to extend their children's social and economic opportunities, though it should be added that the Irish primary and grammar schools were consistently more crowded than their Yankee counterparts (the Irish schools were actually publicly supported parochial schools during the

[7] The phrase "city of spindles" is from the labor newspaper *The Voice of Industry*, November 7, 1845.

1840s and early 1850s, under a local political arrangement widely referred to as the Lowell plan) and that only a small number of Irish youngsters went on to the high school. Finally, we know that only a handful of workers in Lowell's factories were under the age of fifteen. Apparently, the holding power of the public schools was substantial, particularly as aided by a vigorous campaign against truancy after 1842.

Once the young women entered the mills, there began another phase of their education that is important to delineate. (I am using the term "education" to refer only to those aspects of socialization to factory routine that were deliberate, systematic, and sustained.) In the first place, there was education in work skills and routines, overseen by the owners and the managers. The process was one of apprenticeship, in which the newcomer worked initially as a sparehand in collaboration with a more experienced partner, gradually "learning by doing," later spelling either the partner or some absentee for brief periods of time, and eventually taking on a regular job. As one operative described it in *The Lowell Offering*, "Well, I went into the mill, and was put to learn with a very patient girl. . . . They set me to threading shuttles, and tying weaver's knots, and such things, and now I have improved so that I can take care of one loom. I could take care of two if only I had eyes in the back part of my head." But there was also the education of the dormitories, overseen, to be sure, by the owners and their employed housekeepers but increasingly teaching group norms and standards enforced by peer pressures revolving around acceptance and shunning. The romantic literature on Lowell celebrated the uplifting thrust of these pressures in enforcing high standards of moral conduct; but, as Thomas Dublin has pointed out, it was these very pressures that helped weld the young women into a cohesive group of strikers in 1834 and 1836. Finally, it is important to recall that the factory operatives remained in close touch with their familial households; indeed, relationships of kith and kin were often central in determining patterns of recruitment to and departure from the mills. They also partook with the townspeople of the education offered by churches, Sunday schools, evening schools, libraries, lyceums, and voluntary associations. And they read newspapers—their own, initially *The Lowell Offering* and later *The Voice of Industry*, as well as local papers such as *The Lowell Journal* and Boston papers such as *The Evening Transcript*. In sum, the mills and their attached dormitories served as mediating agencies for the operatives' education during their membership in the work force; but it would be quite inaccurate to portray them as "total institutions." Later, when the dormitories disappeared and the mills began to recruit a very different kind of work force and maintained a very different kind of work relationship, the generalization remained valid.[8]

Sumter District, South Carolina, presents a quite different set of educational configurations. The district, situated in the

---

[8] *The Lowell Offering*, 4 (1844): 170; and Thomas Louis Dublin, "Women at Work: The Transformation of Work and Community in Lowell, Massachusetts, 1826–1860" (unpublished doctoral thesis, Columbia University, 1975). John F. Kasson applies the concept of the "total institution" to pre–Civil War Lowell in *Civilizing the Machine: Technology and Republican Values in America, 1776–1900* (New York: Grossman Publishers, 1976), chap. 2.

fertile plains of the upper pine belt some forty miles east of the city of Columbia, was created by the state legislature on January 1, 1800. The principal dynamic of its economic life during the first half of the nineteenth century was the boom in cotton cultivation following the invention of the cotton gin and the subsequent development of cotton as a staple money crop. Since Sumter's geographic boundaries changed several times during the nineteenth century, it is difficult to obtain demographic statistics that are comparable over time; the best estimates place the population at 13,103 in 1800, 28,277 in 1830, 23,859 in 1860 (the decline owing to the creation of Clarendon County in 1855, part of which was taken from Sumter District), and 25,268 in 1870. The black population increased both absolutely and proportionally during this period, from 6,864, or 52 percent, in 1800 to 17,002, or 71 percent, in 1860, with the overwhelming majority of the blacks having unfree status. As was true throughout the South, most white families in Sumter did not own slaves, and most of those white families that did own slaves owned ten or fewer. Only 2 percent of the Sumter slaveholders in 1850 actually owned a hundred or more slaves, but their plantations accounted for a significant fraction of the total slave population of the district, perhaps as much as 25 percent.[9]

[9] The chief secondary works relating to Sumter District are Rosser H. Taylor, *Ante-Bellum South Carolina: A Social and Cultural History* (Chapel Hill: University of North Carolina Press, 1942), Anne King Gregorie, *History of Sumter County, South Carolina* (Sumter, S.C.: Library Board of Sumter County, 1954), Janie Revill, *Sumter District* (No place: The State Printing Company, 1968), and Chalmers Gaston Davidson, *The Last Foray: The South Carolina Planters of 1860, A Sociological Study* (Columbia: University of South Carolina Press, 1971). The statistics are drawn from the federal census, the acts and resolutions of the South Carolina General As-

Prior to the Revolution, there were three churches in Sumter, St. Mark's Church (Anglican), Black River Church (Presbyterian), and High Hills Church (Baptist). Between the Revolution and the Civil War, additional churches were established in several ways. Some, like the Bethel Baptist Church of Claremont, split off from established institutions, in that instance, the High Hills Baptist Church. Some developed in the wake of Methodist circuit riders, such as Francis Asbury, who first visited the region in 1785, and James Jenkins, who began riding what was called the Santee Circuit in 1795. And a few grew up in connection with some specific ethnic group, for example, the Roman Catholic church in Sumterville, organized to serve the town's Irish population. A map of the district drawn in the early 1820s indicates at least twenty-six separate church buildings, but the number of congregations was probably higher, since there were almost surely congregations without permanent quarters. A half-century later, the census of 1870 reported some forty congregations, including nineteen Methodist, nine Baptist, eight Presbyterian, three Episcopalian, and one Roman Catholic. By that time, too, there were numerous auxiliary agencies, such as the Sumter Bible Society, the YMCA, the annual Methodist camp meeting, and a variety of libraries and Sunday schools that had developed in connection with the several churches.

The first schools in Sumter also emerged in connection with the churches. Even before the Revolution, the ministers of the Black River Church and St. Mark's Church conducted

---

sembly, and, beginning in 1869, the annual reports of the state superintendent of education.

regular classes, and there is evidence of "old-field schools" that convened in abandoned log cabins. From an early date, there were also academies, such as the Claremont Academy in Stateburg, which opened in 1786, closed in 1788, and then reopened in 1819. Like Claremont, most of the academies enjoyed brief or intermittent lives, and it is virtually impossible to determine how many of them actually existed at any given time. Since academy curricula usually depended in part on the particular students who happened to be enrolled, it is also difficult to generalize about what subjects were offered, though it is likely that most of the institutions provided opportunities to go beyond the three R's. Some of the academies were teacher-owned, some were organized by parents, and some were incorporated by "societies" of one sort or another. A family might send its son to the Sumter Military, Gymnastic, and Classical School to obtain a combination of "academical learning" and the "manly arts," or it might send its daughter to Mrs. Campbell's School for Young Ladies to study geography, astronomy, embroidery, needlework, and the social graces.

With the exception of a few elite institutions that managed to attract state-wide clienteles, Sumter's academies did not cater to either the highest or the lowest classes of white society, and certainly not to any portion of black society. Wealthier parents tended to have their children tutored at home, while poorer parents desirous of schooling for their youngsters sent them to the public schools organized under the Free School Law of 1811. By 1826, Sumter District had forty-three such public schools enrolling 289 youngsters; by 1853, with a much larger white population, there were sixty-five public schools enrolling 442 youngsters; and by 1860, there were seventy-four public schools enrolling 844 youngsters. Given the provision in the law of 1811 that, in localities where more children applied for public schooling than could be accommodated, first preference would go to the poor and orphaned, there was a continuing stigma attached to attendance at public schools, and they were never on a par with the academies in prestige or quality. In general, there was less schoolgoing among white children in Sumter District than in contemporary northern or midwestern communities, though not as much less as traditional historians of education have inferred by looking only at the records of public-school attendance.

Sumter District also offered a number of opportunities for systematic self-education. By 1809, both Stateburg and Sumterville had circulating libraries, and by 1855 Sumterville also boasted its own bookstore. There were numerous agricultural fairs organized by the Sumter Agricultural Association and a variety of traveling medical shows, circuses, and concert troupes. Finally, there were the local newspapers, such as *The Sumter Banner* and *The Watchman*, which actively debated everything from the nullification issue to whether it was proper for a perfect gentleman to pick his teeth at the table or wipe his mouth with the tablecloth.

All these opportunities were for whites only. Even for free blacks, the chance to participate in church activities was at best restricted, and their access to formal schooling was actually prohibited by law after 1834. For the slaves, the differences were even more drastic. In the smaller slave-owning households, black youngsters might spend their earliest years in close and continuing association with their white agemates; but when they reached seven or eight their paths would diverge, with the black youngsters' education thereafter restricted to whatever might come from marginal participation in the church or apprenticeship to some adult artisan. Some did learn to read and write, but informally, alongside their white agemates, and, after 1834, more and more clandestinely. In the larger slave-owning households, there was an even wider bifurcation along racial lines. Once again, a few black youngsters might spend their earliest years in close and continuing association with their white agemates, but they would more likely remain in a segregated company of blacks, overseen by older members of the quarter-community itself. Meanwhile, the white youngsters would be tutored at home, the males in preparation for one of the elite academies in the state, for example, the Mount Zion Society School at Winnsborough, or Beaufort College, or the College of South Carolina, or the College of Charleston, the females perhaps in preparation for a school such as the Bradford Springs Female Institute or the Harmony Female College, both located in Sumter. The owners, overseers, and slaves of some plantations worshiped together in nearby churches or residential establishments, with the slaves grouped in special pews in the rear; elsewhere, segregated services for blacks were conducted by local or itinerant Methodist or Baptist preachers. Beyond that, and it is an important generalization to bear in mind, most of the education blacks received came from the quarter-community itself, from black households and black clandestine congregations transmitting an eclectic culture of black folklore, agricultural and artisan skills, a version of Christianity, and the remembered experience of accommodation and protest.

Macoupin County, Illinois, provides yet another story. Located roughly sixty miles northeast of St. Louis, between Madison County, which borders on Missouri, and Sangamon County, which includes Springfield, Macoupin furnishes a useful laboratory for studying the educational configurations of the nineteenth-century frontier. The first settlers came to Macoupin in the 1810s, but as late as 1817 the county could boast only five families. During the next decade immigration to the county increased steadily though slowly, with most of the settlers coming from the southern states, especially Kentucky, the Carolinas, Tennessee, Virginia, and Georgia. The population was about two thousand in 1830, slightly over twelve thousand in 1850, and almost thirty-three thousand in 1870, with small numbers of free blacks present from 1830 on and with relatively small proportions of foreign-born—the percentage was 17.4 in 1860 and 14.6 in 1870. [10]

What we know of Macoupin's churches tends to support William Warren Sweet's thesis, especially as restated by Donald Mathews, namely, that the churches tamed and disciplined the frontier; though it is difficult to obtain precise figures on the number of people who actually attended those churches. The Methodists and the Baptists were the first to arrive—they could boast seven churches each in 1850, thirteen

[10] The chief secondary work is *History of Macoupin County, Illinois* (Philadelphia: Brink, McDonough & Company, 1879). The statistics are drawn from the federal census and the reports of the state superintendent of public instruction.

and seventeen, respectively, in 1860, and twenty-five and twenty in 1870. The Presbyterians were right behind, with two churches in 1850, eleven in 1860, and ten in 1870. And there were also small numbers of Congregational, Lutheran, and Roman Catholic churches. Relative to the total population, Macoupin had one church for every six hundred people in 1850, one for every five hundred in 1860, and one for every four hundred in 1870; though it is probable that at no time did more than a quarter of the population have any formal church connection, and it is difficult in any case to determine the nature, intensity, and effects of church affiliations among those who did maintain them. Certainly one indication of change over time is the fact that the leading religious issue of the 1830s was irreligion, the leading religious issue of the 1850s doctrinal orthodoxy, and the leading religious issue of the 1870s institution building, especially the building of Lutheran and Catholic parochial schools.[11]

There is early evidence of a school at the county seat of Carlinville, where the Methodist circuit rider Stith Otwell and his wife Mary lived when they first arrived in 1831. We also know, from a reminiscence Mrs. Otwell left in 1870 under the name Mrs. Mary Byram Wright, that schooling in Carlinville was offered not only in the schoolhouse but in every manner of public and private building; conversely, the house the Otwells later built for themselves served not only as their residence but also as the county surveyor's office, the post office,

[11] William Warren Sweet, *Religion in the Development of American Culture, 1765–1840* (New York: Charles Scribner's Sons, 1952), pp. 153–154; and Donald G. Mathews, "The Second Great Awakening as an Organizing Process, 1780–1830: An Hypothesis," *American Quarterly*, 21 (1969): 23–45.

and a dry-goods store—interestingly, church services were not ordinarily held there, since all the denominations used the county courthouse for that purpose during the 1830s. Thus, the doubling up or tripling up of functions that had manifested itself in seventeenth-century Virginia appears to have been a continuing phenomenon of frontier development. Buildings served multiple purposes and people played multiple roles. In any case, to look directly at the school statistics for 1850 and 1870 is to come yet again upon arresting data indicating that schooling, of some indeterminate kind and duration, was well-nigh universal from the earliest years of midwestern development. Thus, the census of 1850 reported the existence of seventy-two public schools in Macoupin County taught by seventy-three teachers and enrolling 1,958 pupils. Moreover, the same census reported 3,365 youngsters in school attendance. Now, the discrepancy between the figures for school attendance and public-school enrollment was common in the census of 1850, and in Macoupin County as in many other places the larger figure doubtless included youngsters attending private schools, Sunday schools, and quasi schools of every sort and variety. What is important about mid-century Macoupin is that some 90 percent of a total population of 3,695 between the ages of five and fourteen was spending some time in some kind of school, and this fully five years before the Illinois legislature established a state-wide, tax-supported, public-school system. By 1870, the school attendance figure was 8,201, of a total population of 10,953 between the ages of five and eighteen; but by this time public schooling accounted for most of that number. Incidentally, Macoupin also boasted its own institution of higher learning, called Blackburn University. Characteristically for the era and the region, it had originated out of a combination of boosterism and religiosity, under the sponsorship of a Presbyterian minister-entrepreneur named Gideon Blackburn. By 1870, it already had a preparatory department, a full collegiate department, and a theological department, and the first college class was graduated that year, with seven students proceeding A.B.[12]

Finally, there were three jails, a poor farm, a variety of voluntary associations affiliated with the churches, and several newspapers—some, like *The Staunton Banner*, proving ephemeral, others, like *The Carlinville Free Democrat*, more permanent. The latter newspaper was for all intents and purposes a carbon copy of Horace Greeley's *Tribune*, differing only in size and geographical focus. It used all of Greeley's pedagogical devices, from the featuring of editorials to the personification of issues (Polk's war, Douglas's bill, Taney's decision); and, like many a newspaper of the time, it virtually ignored local news, apparently believing that no one would really pay for information that could be obtained by word of mouth from neighbors.[13]

Now, what can we say of the ways in which particular individuals came to the educational opportunities in Lowell, Sumter, and Macoupin? Once again, we have at hand a few

[12] Mrs. Mary Byram Wright, "Personal Recollections of the Early Settlement of Carlinville, Illinois," *Journal of the Illinois Historical Society*, 18 (1925–26): 668–685.
[13] Everett R. Turnbull, "A Century of Methodism in Carlinville, Illinois," *Journal of the Illinois State Historical Society*, 24 (1931–32): 259. See also Milton W. Hamilton, *The Country Printer: New York State, 1785–1830* (New York: Columbia University Press, 1936), p. 139.

examples, none of which ought to be generalized. There is, first of all, the familiar story of Lucy Larcom, probably the best known of the early factory operatives in Lowell. The daughter of a sea captain in Beverly, Massachusetts, Lucy Larcom grew up in a pleasant ambience bounded by household, church, school, and local community. She claimed she learned to read at the age of two, from her father and her Aunt Lucy, who lived nearby; from a kind and motherly teacher called "Aunt Hannah," who presided over informal classes in her kitchen and sitting room above Captain Larcom's shop and from whom Lucy also learned spinning and the New Testament; and from her pastor, whom she visited with her family on Sundays. Lucy also recalled Captain Larcom's insistence that all the children, girls as well as boys, develop some independent means of support "by the labor of their hands." [14]

Captain Larcom died when Lucy was seven, and Lucy's mother moved the family to Lowell, where she took a job as a housekeeper in one of the factory-connected dormitories, while Lucy and her younger sister attended the town grammar school and the older girls went to work in the factory. Lucy herself later went to work at the mills, spending ten years living in a typical factory boardinghouse. Newly built of red brick, it quickly filled with "a large feminine family," numbering probably twenty to thirty. Most of the boarders came from New Hampshire and Vermont, and "there was a fresh, breezy sociability about them"; they slept several to a room, waking

---

[14] Lucy Larcom, *A New England Girlhood* (New York: Corinth Books, 1961), pp. 39, 121. See also Daniel Dulany Addison, *Lucy Larcom: Life, Letters, and Diary* (Boston: Houghton, Mifflin and Company, 1894).

before dawn and hurrying to the mills before the gates closed at five. The dining room, where lunch and supper were served, doubled as a sitting room in the evenings, when the girls gathered around the bare tables sewing, talking, or reading. Often, newsboys, shoe dealers, booksellers, and the like interrupted the leisure hours. Remembering one such evening, Larcom later wrote:

> A pedlar came in while they stayed, whose wares
> The girls sat cheapening. A phrenologist
> Displaced the pedlar, and the tide of mirth
> Flowed in around the tables, as he read
> The cranial character of each to each.

In addition to receiving informal education from pedlars and phrenologists, the young women attended lyceum lectures, where they heard such speakers as Edward Everett, Ralph Waldo Emerson, and John Quincy Adams; they took part in dozens of discussion and study groups, both inside and outside the dormitories; and they studied everything from German to Chaucer to botany in night classes taught by "literary ladies." Lucy left Lowell in 1845 and went west with her sister Emilie's new family, teaching in a district school for a time and then enrolling in the Monticello Female Seminary—"one of the best in the country," as she put it, and "certainly second to none in the West." She went on to write poetry, to lecture, to teach at Wheaton Seminary in Massachusetts, to edit a children's magazine, and, finally, to achieve modest fame when *A New England Girlhood* appeared in 1889.[15]

[15] Larcom, *New England Girlhood*, pp. 152, 265; and Lucy Larcom, *An Idyl of Work* (Boston: James R. Osgood and Company, 1875), p. 96.

What is one to make of this, particularly in the sketchy form in which I have presented it? Several things, I would hope. First, to contemplate Larcom's girlhood in Beverly is to be cautioned against easy generalizations regarding the total or decisive influence of the factory experience. The mills and their boardinghouses were influential, to be sure, but the particular education each young woman brought to the mill experience inevitably shaped both the manner in which she underwent and responded to that experience and the nature of the experience that would follow. Lucy Larcom's life was simply different from that of Harriet Robinson, who was descended from an old Boston family and who went on to become a leader in the women's suffrage movement, and from that of Sarah G. Bagley, who came from New Hampshire and ended up as a full-time labor organizer for the Female Labor Reform Association. And it was even more different from that of Margaret Baxter, an Irish immigrant who went to work in the mills in 1849 and advanced rather quickly because she had learned to read, and from that of Catherine Matthews, also an Irish immigrant who went to work in the mills in 1849 but who began as a sweeper and remained a sweeper for more than a decade, owing partly to the fact that she was illiterate. To repeat an earlier assertion, the education of the factory mediated other educative influences, but it neither replaced them nor rendered them ineffectual.[16]

We are fortunate in having two extant slave narratives de-

[16] I am grateful to Thomas Dublin for the information on Margaret Baxter and Catherine Matthews, which is taken from unpublished data he gathered in connection with the preparation of "Women at Work." Dublin's monograph presents a group portrait of the operatives between 1826 and 1860.

scribing life in Sumter District, one by Jacob Stroyer and one by Irving E. Lowery. The two men were born on plantations less than twenty miles apart, Stroyer in 1849 and Lowery in 1850. After emancipation, they both became ministers in the Methodist Episcopal church, which identifies them, incidentally, as anything but ordinary; yet their reminiscences tell us much about the dynamics of education, and miseducation, as they proceeded under slavery.[17]

Jacob Stroyer grew up on one of the several Singleton family plantations in the southwest corner of Sumter District, some twenty-eight miles from Columbia. His master, Matthew R. Singleton, was the second son of Colonel Richard Singleton, who had originally amassed the lands and the fortune they represented. While the chief crop was cotton, one gleans from the narrative the remarkable range of agricultural, manufacturing, and recreational activities that took place on the plantation—including horse racing, in which Stroyer became involved as a jockey. In all, there were some four hundred slaves in Matthew Singleton's establishment, who formed the substantial quarter-community within which Stroyer came of age.

Four educational themes emerge from Stroyer's autobiography: his own growing personal strength and self-respect; the capricious but inexorable cruelty of the white world; the vitality of the quarter-community, and particularly of Stroyer's immediate family; and the opportunities for self-education via the church, especially after emancipation. Stroyer's narrative

[17] Jacob Stroyer, *My Life in the South* (4th ed.; Salem, Mass.: Newcomb & Gauss, 1898); and I. E. Lowery, *Life on the Old Plantation in Ante-Bellum Days* (Columbia, S.C.: The State Company, 1911).

begins, "My father was born in Sierra Leone, Africa." The sentence is a fitting introduction, for Stroyer admired his father, deliberately modeled himself after him, and was able clearly to distinguish between the man, whom he loved, and the slave role that the man had been forced to assume. Stroyer's father was not a field hand; he took care of the hogs and cows and, in later years, of the horses and mules. While still a young boy, Stroyer began to help his father at the "occupation of hostler," which for the first time brought him into direct personal contact with the cruel realities of the slave system. [18]

Prior to the time he learned to ride, Stroyer's life had been centered in the quarter-community. He spent summers at the Sand Hill (the Singleton's "summer seat," four miles from the main plantation) with the other slave children who were too young to work. The food was unpalatable but the discipline was lax; three or four older black women cared for the eighty to a hundred fifty youngsters who roamed freely in the woods, being interrupted only occasionally to be scrubbed for some forthcoming visit of the master and mistress. Winters were spent on the plantation proper, though Stroyer tells us little of the diurnal routines there. What does emerge clearly is that the relative integrity of his family life, as evidenced by strict rules about going to bed early, prohibitions against joining in adult conversation, and requirements concerning nightly family prayer, along with the embedment of that family life in a community in which children addressed adults as uncle and aunt, gave Stroyer a sense of personal security that was to en-

[18] Stroyer, *My Life in the South*, pp. 7, 17.

dure despite the harsh lessons administered by the white community. For Stroyer, the family performed a decisive mediative function. It could not protect him from abuse, but it could impose meaning on that abuse, thereby minimizing the damage it inflicted.

From the time he began to ride, while still too small to do so, to the time he gave it up because he had become too heavy, Stroyer was subjected to relentless physical cruelty. He was whipped when he climbed onto a horse, he was whipped when he fell off a horse, and he was whipped for no reason at all; and, when he was badly hurt by a horse that stepped on his cheek, he was not even given the day off. Although he came slowly to the realization that his "dear father and mother" and the rest of his "fellow Negroes" were utterly defenseless in the face of harsh mistreatment, he received comfort from his father's prayers for his children's liberation and from his parents' pride in his skill as a jockey. By the time he reached his early teens, Stroyer had somehow learned to read; he had formed an aspiration to become a "famous carpenter"; he had manifested an ability to decide when to submit to and when to resist white authority; and he had even demonstrated the capability of sabotaging the plans of his supervisors. Not surprisingly, Matthew Singleton's overseer had already identified young Jacob as a dangerous influence; and, had the Civil War not intervened, he would most likely have become an exceedingly troublesome slave. [19]

During the war, Stroyer spent a year working on the fortifications at Sullivan's Island, near Charleston, and was

[19] *Ibid.*, pp. 18, 32.

wounded by gunfire at Fort Sumter. Although he was still enslaved and living amidst other uneducated blacks, Stroyer was at least free enough from constant surveillance to pursue his education openly—indeed, he remarks that he even studied his spelling book while under bombardment from Northern guns. Obviously, his early experience had given him sufficient self-respect to reach through the smallest cracks in the wall of oppression that stood between him and the freedom that he (and his father) craved. After emancipation, Stroyer made his way north to New England, where he studied for a time in the evening schools of Worcester, Massachusetts, and obtained a license as a local preacher for the African Methodist Episcopal church. At the time he published his autobiography in 1879, he was seeking funds for the continuation of his theological studies at Talladega College in Alabama; and, while the narrative is decidedly colored by that purpose, its value and authenticity remain considerable.

The stark brutalities that pepper the Stroyer narrative are virtually absent from the account of his contemporary Irving E. Lowery. Lowery pointedly wrote his reminiscences as a "record of the better life of those days," as an effort to balance accounts (like Stroyer's) that focused on the "evil side." Although it is possible that the slaves on John Frierson's plantation in the southeastern part of Sumter District were consistently better treated than those on the Singleton plantations—for one thing, there were only forty-five of them in the Frierson establishment, which surely made a difference—Lowery's account indicates that it may have been his close and continuing personal association with the Frierson

77

family that blinded him to the harsher realities of what he called "life on the old plantation." [20]

There is little about Lowery's parents in the narrative. They were mulattoes and they felt close to the Friersons, and that is all we are told. At an early age, Lowery became Mr. Frierson's waiting boy and moved into the plantation house itself, away from his kin. He ate and slept in the Frierson house, accompanied Frierson on his social and business calls, and even participated with the Friersons in their evening prayers; and, although he did play with other slave boys and at times had to work in the fields, Lowery readily admitted that he was "something of a privileged character." Obviously cut off from the culture of the quarter-community and obviously the recipient of consistently kind and special treatment, Lowery experienced an education that was dominated by the instruction of the white household. [21]

Virtually all of Lowery's anecdotes recount aspects of the white pedagogy he accepted without reservation. Frierson took his slaves to Sunday school and services at the Shiloh Methodist Church at least once a month, and he also employed a black preacher to instruct them on the plantation. He did so, according to Lowery, "to keep the slaves—and especially the younger ones—out of mischief," to ensure their spiritual and moral uplift, and to keep them from desecrating God's holy day. The preachers Frierson employed made a "deep impression," if not on the entire assemblage at least on Lowery himself—he was actually able to recall verbatim a sermon he had

[20] Lowery, *Life on the Old Plantation*, p. 10.
[21] *Ibid.*, pp. 100, 103.

once heard as a boy on the theme that running away is a sin that cannot be hidden from God.[22]

Lowery's account of "life on the old plantation" may be a great deal rosier than the actuality, even granting that Frierson was a model slaveowner. But there is no reason to discount his narrative completely as mere exaggeration. Lowery was only too aware that Frierson was not a typical master and that he himself was not a typical slave, and indeed that, despite Frierson's continuing efforts, others of his slaves stole, ran away, and even murdered. The narrative simply attests to the power of white pedagogy when it was not undermined, either by anomalous white cruelty or by contradictory black teaching emanating from the quarter-community. In fact, it is a poignant irony that shortly after emancipation Lowery was actually beaten by Frierson's son for becoming too "frolicsome" during the course of some work in the fields, and as a result Lowery left the plantation in a rage to work with his father on a rented farm nearby. It was then, at the age of sixteen, that he began to study at a free school for blacks sponsored by a New England missionary society, thereby launching his post–Civil War career as pastor and teacher.

Lowery had experienced a profoundly different education from Stroyer's; yet each had emerged from the slave experience with a sufficient sense of personal integrity to make effective use of educational opportunities that became available after the achievement of freedom. Others among their contemporaries, some of whom appear ephemerally on the margins of their accounts, were less fortunate: Josh, the joke-

[22] *Ibid.*, pp. 70, 80.

ster who stole from his fellow slaves; Aunt Betty and Granny the cook, who were devoted house servants; Monday and Jim, who were able field hands; Cyrus and Stepney, who resisted an overseer and were lynched summarily when the overseer died mysteriously a few days later. The education of such individuals cannot be detailed and indeed will never be known in its particulars; but for that very reason it ought not to be described with overly facile generalizations. John W. Blassingame, Eugene D. Genovese, and Thomas Lane Webber have recently given us carefully drawn collective biographies of pre–Civil War slaves; and what is abundantly clear from their studies is that slave education was a complex phenomenon involving different combinations of black and white pedagogy transmitted via different configurations of household, church, and school. As in the case of Lucy Larcom and the other factory operatives in Lowell, it is important, in attempting to understand the education of the slaves, neither to overgeneralize from a few extant autobiographies nor to oversimplify regarding the "inevitable" effects of some theoretically constructed "total institution." [23]

There are at least two persons whose lives are similarly instructive with respect to nineteenth-century Macoupin County. The first is John McAuley Palmer, who was governor of Illinois from 1868 to 1872; the second is the Reverend

[23] John W. Blassingame, *The Slave Community: Plantation Life in the Ante-Bellum South* (New York: Oxford University Press, 1972); Eugene D. Genovese, *Roll, Jordan, Roll: The World the Slaves Made* (New York: Pantheon Books, 1974); and Webber, "Education of the Slave Quarter Community." The portrayal of slavery as a "total institution" is given in R. S. Bryce-Laporte, *American Slave Plantations as Total Institutions* (New York: Allyn and Bacon, 1970) and criticized in Blassingame, *Slave Community*, pp. 217–226.

James Henry Magee, a free black whose odyssey led him through Macoupin for a time and who eventually settled in Cincinnati as pastor of the United Baptist church there. Palmer was born in southern Kentucky in 1817, to a cabinetmaker of Scotch-Irish descent and Baptist persuasion. He recalled his father as an omnivorous reader who "made himself familiar with the meager political literature of the day and became an admirer and devoted adherent of Mr. Jefferson." Apparently, there was a good deal of political education in the Palmer household. In addition, there was the common recollection of having early learned to read and having attended school to study the "essential branches of education as they were then understood—reading, writing and arithmetic as far as the 'rule of three.' " The family moved to Illinois in 1829, where John worked for five years on a farm his father purchased in Madison County, west of Macoupin. In 1834—recall that John was then seventeen—his father offered him the opportunity to seek further schooling, provided he support himself. There followed another five-year period in which he alternated between school, work, and school-*cum*-work (with a period of attendance at Alton College, one of the early manual labor institutions in Illinois); and then, in 1839, John went to Macoupin County to live with his brother Elihu, who was pastor of the Baptist church in Carlinville. The rest of the story sounds like a life of Abraham Lincoln. Palmer went to study in the office of John S. Greathouse, a Carlinville attorney, and read law as well as English history and other relevant subjects under Greathouse's tutelage. In less than a year, he was admitted to the bar, and in 1840 he began a political career that led to a divisional command in the Northern armies during the Civil War and then to the statehouse.[24]

What we know of Magee comes largely from an autobiography entitled *The Night of Affliction and Morning of Recovery*, published in 1873. He was born in Madison County in 1839, of a free black father and a slave mother who had been purchased by his father in order that he might marry her. The family moved to Macoupin County in 1845, where James's father bought a small farm and where James and his brother attended the Merryweather district school for a time and then a private "colored" school conducted by a Mrs. Daniel Barton. After further schooling in Racine, Wisconsin, Magee returned to Macoupin, where he taught for a number of years. In 1863 he was ordained a Baptist minister and embarked upon a pastoral career that subsequently took him to further study in London, to the principalship of a Baptist college in Nashville, to engagement in politics, to participation in the founding of the Illinois Colored Historical Society, and to the pastorship of the First Baptist Church in Cincinnati.[25]

Once again, one cannot generalize from two sketchy educational biographies. What does become clear is that individuals made their own way, irregularly, intermittently, and indeterminately, through the educational configurations of the nineteenth-century frontier, going back and forth across the per-

[24] *Personal Recollections of John M. Palmer: The Story of an Earnest Life* (Cincinnati: The Robert Clarke Company, 1901), pp. 2, 4. See also George Thomas Palmer, *A Conscientious Turncoat: The Story of John M. Palmer, 1817–1900* (New Haven: Yale University Press, 1941).

[25] J. H. Magee, *The Night of Affliction and Morning of Recovery: An Autobiography* (Cincinnati: Published by the author, 1873).

meable boundaries of household, church, school, and apprenticeship, largely self-motivated and largely self-directed toward particular goals. Some were cut off and some were constrained, to be sure; but again, to see the household or the church or the school or the work situation in isolation as "total" or decisive is to misread the history of the era.

III

MY ARGUMENT has been that an authentic American vernacular in education emerged during the first century of national life, that the vernacular incarnated and advanced the notion of a popular *paideia* in the making, and that the commitment of the vernacular was the creation of a new republican individual of virtuous character, abiding patriotism, and prudent wisdom, fit to develop a favored nation whose Great Seal proclaimed to the world Virgil's aphorism, *novus ordo seclorum*, "a new order of the ages." How did this vernacular in education relate to what we might think of as the characteristically American in other realms of life?

Several possibilities come to mind, on several levels of generalization. First, those who have written about vernaculars in the past, mostly in the realm of the arts and language, have tended to be apologists for uniqueness: they have argued that what is characteristically American grew out of the American soil, so to speak, in response to American needs and in the context of American conditions, and that hence the vernacular is in its very nature *sui generis*. I should therefore say at the outset that I see no inconsistency between my argument that an authentic American vernacular in education emerged and the assertion that the vernacular was not unique. One of the most important things we are relearning from the work of Brian Simon, Harold Silver, John F. C. Harrison, and E. G. West, to mention but four recent students of nineteenth-century English education, is that the popularization of education was a general Western, not a uniquely American, phenomenon, and that the principal figures in the movement on both sides of the Atlantic were in constant communication. Thus, Methodist, Owenite, and Lancasterian ideas and strategies deeply affected American education during the first half of the nineteenth century, while the American experience was itself known and variously interpreted by Englishmen during the latter half. Or, to take another example, the development of rehabilitative and custodial institutions such as the asylum, the reformatory, and the penitentiary was a transatlantic phenomenon in which Europeans and Americans exchanged both ideas and models. The movement may have found fertile soil in Jacksonian America, as David Rothman has indicated, but it was neither uniquely Jacksonian nor uniquely American. What is different, perhaps, about the nineteenth century is the shift in the balance of the exchange, from American dependence during the colonial era to a more symmetrical give-and-take relationship. Recall that Frances Trollope's report on the domestic manners of the Americans, Philip Schaff's report on the churches of America, Francis Adams's report on the schools of America, and Gustave de Beaumont's and Alexis de Tocqueville's report on the prisons of America were avidly read in Europe, and there was a good deal of style-setting eastward that was of a different order from the seventeenth-century romanticizing of the noble savages or the eighteenth-century lionizing of Franklin in his fur cap.[26]

I would submit further that the new vernaculars of American education and the popularization they made possible moved American education, on balance, in the direction of increased diversity and choice. The important phrase, of course, is "on balance"; for there is abundant evidence that families, churches, schools, and colleges continued to try to form youngsters along particular lines, and that newspapers continued to propound particular ideologies. But one need not deny the fact that groups used education for the purpose of social control to affirm the equally important fact that the multitude of groups doing so, and the greater availability of diverse options that resulted from their efforts, extended the range of choice for individuals. If nothing else, the intellectual and social literacy fostered by the churches and schools (by which I mean the near-universal ability to read, write, and in-

[26] Brian Simon, *Studies in the History of Education, 1780–1870* (London: Lawrence & Wishart, 1960); Harold Silver, *The Concept of Popular Education: A Study of Ideas and Social Movements in the Early Nineteenth Century* (London: Macgibbon & Kee, 1965); John F. C. Harrison, *Quest for the New Moral World: Robert Owen and the Owenites in Britain and America* (New York: Charles Scribner's Sons, 1969); E. G. West, *Education and the Industrial Revolution* (New York: Barnes & Noble, 1975); Frances Trollope, *Domestic Manners of the Americans* (1832; reprint ed.; New York: Dodd, Mead & Company, 1927); Philip Schaff, *America: A Sketch of the Political, Social, and Religious Character of the United States of North America* (New York: C. Scribner, 1855); Francis Adams, *The Free School System of the United States* (London: Chapman and Hall, 1875); and Gustave de Beaumont and Alexis de Tocqueville, *On the Penitentiary System of the United States, and Its Application in France*, translated by Francis Lieber (Philadelphia: Carey, Lea & Blanchard, 1833).

teract with individuals who were not kin) afforded people the possibility of release from geographical and social place, and in so doing augmented personal liberty. The caveat needs reiteration: the vernaculars did not necessarily augment liberty for the slaves, or for the Indians, or for the voluntarily or involuntarily segregated, or for those who failed to perceive the opportunities or who were prevented from taking advantage of them; but these inexcusable omissions must not obscure the extension of opportunity for many others beyond what they might have enjoyed earlier or elsewhere.

By advancing liberty, the vernaculars of American education also advanced equality, at least in the sense in which the term was used during the nineteenth century. They afforded more varied and extensive opportunities for education to many who had previously enjoyed rather limited opportunities, thereby broadening access to life chances that had formerly been confined to the few. One need not argue that Blackburn University was the equal of Harvard College to grant that the United States of 1870 with five hundred colleges had moved considerably beyond the America of 1776 with nine colleges or the England of 1870 with three universities. And one need not deny the continuing influence of ability, wealth, status, and luck to affirm the role of education in facilitating access to positions of prestige, influence, and personal fulfillment— Lucy Larcom's career in teaching and letters, John McAuley Palmer's in law and politics, and Jacob Stroyer's, Irving E. Lowery's, and James Henry Magee's in the ministry are all cases in point. Indeed, the very nature of such positions was inextricably tied to the expansion of education: not only were increasing numbers of such positions coming to have educational requirements for initial entry and advancement, but education was itself helping to create more and more such positions.

Finally, the vernaculars of American education sought to provide a sense of community for a people who were increasing in number, diversifying in origin, and insistently mobile. Granting that the *paideia* that emerged was never static, and that it varied significantly from place to place, I believe it may be fairly characterized as a Christian *paideia* that united the symbols of Protestantism, the values of the New Testament, *Poor Richard's Almanack*, and the *Federalist* papers, and the aspirations asserted on the Great Seal. It was a national *paideia* too; and, though it could not transcend the social, political, and intellectual divisiveness that culminated in the Civil War, it did come to the fore again during the great centennial celebration of 1876. Indeed, I would consider that coming to the fore a more auspicious event in the history of the Republic than President Hayes's order a year later removing the last of the army of occupation from the South. For the intellectual drawing together of 1876 was needed before the peace of 1877, such as it was, could be achieved. Whether or not, as Emerson once forecast, the time will come when education supersedes politics as the fundamental mode of human affairs, education has already preceded and set the stage for politics at several critical turning points in the nation's history.[27]

[27] Ralph Waldo Emerson, "Culture" (1860), *The Complete Essays and Other Writings of Ralph Waldo Emerson*, edited by Brooks Atkinson (New York: Random House, 1940), p. 722.

THE METROPOLITAN

EXPERIENCE

1876–1976

THE HOOPLA of 1876 was compounded of the same mixture of pride, pretension, commercialism, cynicism, and shame that marked the hoopla of 1976, with the difference, perhaps, that there was the reality of the great Philadelphia exposition of 1876, which was ultimately attended by one in every five Americans, and there was the general stocktaking that left Grantism behind and set the nation on the road to moral recovery. The preachers, of course, saw it as yet another mark of God's concern for his chosen people. As the liberal minister Horace Bushnell explained it, there had been three definite steps in the evolution of true "nationhood." The first was the Declaration of Independence, which did little more than confirm politically the nation that already existed spiritually. The second was the drafting of the Constitution, which did little more than detail "the constitution already framed by Almighty God in the historic cast of our nation itself." And the third was the testing in the fires of history that was the Civil War, along with the emergence of genuine nationhood that followed, "a sacredly heroic, providentially tragic unity, where God's cherubim stand guard over grudges and hates and remembered jealousies, and the sense of nationality becomes even a kind of religion." America was now free to play its millennial role in history. It remained for the Republic to demonstrate its loyalty to God's example in its national life and in so doing to "give bent to the world's thoughts" and "command its movements." [1]

However exotic the theology accompanying Bushnell's chauvinism, there can be no denying its representativeness. A generation of Protestant preachers from every denomination and every region lectured the United States on its responsibility for righteous world leadership at precisely the time that the United States was beginning to develop the resources with which to attempt it. And the interaction of possibility and aspiration shaped much of the nation's development during the century that followed. I have tended to see metropolitanization as the leitmotif of the era: the United States became an urban nation, in the larger sense in which Lewis Mumford has explicated the term, and the United States at the same time became an exporter of culture and civilization to other parts of the world. And education, in a bewildering variety of

[1] Horace Bushnell, *Building Eras in Religion* (reprint ed.; New York: Charles Scribner's Sons, 1903), pp. 292, 329.

forms and institutions, was profoundly involved in both phe-nomena.[2]

By urbanization, of course, I refer to much more than the simple demographic fact that in 1890 some 30 percent of a population of 63 million lived in cities, in 1920 over half of a population of 106 million lived in cities, in 1950 almost two-thirds of a population of 151 million lived in cities, and in 1970 almost three-quarters of a population of 203 million lived in cities. I refer also to the complex and interrelated phe-nomena we associate with the industrial revolution, the orga-nizational revolution, and the communications revolution of the last century, and even more generally to the phenomenon of modernization. The United States is not only the first mod-ern nation, as has often been remarked, it is also the most modern nation, at least in that semicircuitous logic of the students of modernization, who seem always to define mod-ernization in terms of the social attributes most characteristic of the United States. The point I am making is not merely facetious: there were cities for several thousand years before the appearance of modern industrialism; but, as Mumford has eloquently argued, America has become the quintessential modern metropolitan—or, as he prefers to call it, "megalopol-itan"—civilization.[3]

The demands of a metropolitan civilization upon education are far-reaching. At the very least, they place added burdens on extant institutions, with the result that statements of educa-

[2] Lewis Mumford, *The City in History: Its Origins, Its Transformations, and Its Prospects* (New York: Harcourt, Brace & World, 1961).

[3] *Ibid.*, pp. 555–560.

tional purpose tend significantly to broaden. Thus, to cite several well-known examples from the Progressive era, Washington Gladden summoned the church to extend Christian influence to art, amusement, business, politics, industry, and international relations, indeed to every department of human affairs; John Dewey called upon each school to become an embryonic social community, "active with types of occupations that reflect the life of the larger society, and permeated throughout with the spirit of art, history, and science"; and Walter Lippmann demanded nothing less than a new machinery of knowledge, in which bodies of experts imbued with a selfless equanimity would use the searchlight of reason to enlighten public vision. In place of the self-instructed person of virtuous character, abiding patriotism, and prudent wisdom, the Progressives foresaw the responsible and enlightened citizen informed by the detached and selfless expert, the two in a manifold and lifelong relationship that would involve every institution in every realm of human affairs and ultimately transform all politics into education. "I believe that education is the fundamental method of social progress and reform," Dewey affirmed in his pedagogic creed; ". . . all reforms which rest simply upon the enactment of law, or the threatening of certain penalties, or on changes in mechanical or outward arrangements, are transitory and futile." Whereas Emerson had looked forward to the day when education would supplant politics, Dewey announced that the day had already arrived.[4]

[4] Washington Gladden, *Applied Christianity: The Moral Aspects of Social Questions* (Boston: Houghton, Mifflin and Company, 1886); John Dewey, *The School and*

The other side of metropolitanization involved the deliberate and systematic export of American culture and civilization to other parts of the world. The process assumed a multitude of forms. There was, for example, the Christian missions movement, which began well before the Civil War but which underwent a resurgence during the 1880s and 1890s. The student volunteer movement for Christian missions, formally organized in 1888, announced as its motto "the evangelization of the world in this generation." And President William McKinley explained to some Methodist friends about his change of heart with respect to acquiring the Philippine Islands, "I am not ashamed to tell you, gentlemen, that I went down on my knees and prayed Almighty God for light and guidance more than one night. And one night late it came to me this way—. . . that there was nothing left for us to do but to take them all, and to educate the Filipinos, and uplift and civilize and Christianize them, and by God's grace do the very best we could by them, as our fellow men for whom Christ also died." Imperialism as a policy was compounded of many elements, of which evangelicism was merely one; but that it was, in fact, an aspect of imperialism meant that education would inevitably be involved in dollar diplomacy and direct conquest.[5]

Beyond the missions movement, there was the education implicit in the export, first of manufactured products and later of systems of manufacture themselves. The export of clothing

---

Society (1899), in *Dewey on Education*, edited by Martin S. Dworkin (New York: Teachers College Press, 1959), p. 49; Walter Lippmann, *Public Opinion* (New York: Harcourt, Brace and Company, 1922); and *Dewey on Education*, p. 30.

[5] Charles S. Olcott, *The Life of William McKinley* (2 vols.; Boston: Houghton, Mifflin and Company, 1916), 2:110–111.

offered protection against the elements, but it also furnished instruction in styles of life and costume. The export of automobiles provided transportation, but it also taught design and sooner or later necessitated the training of mechanics. The export of Coca-Cola quenched thirst but it also educated taste and in the process created wants. With some products, as demand rose it became more economical to manufacture them abroad than to export them, and there occurred the export of the factory itself, and with it the rationalized system of production and the concomitant need for trained workers to operate and maintain it. Thus, the export of American know-how followed the export of American products.

Then, too, there was the export of cultural products—books, magazines, and films that instructed directly or entertained and in the process instructed indirectly. And beyond cultural products there was the export of entire systems of education. Kenneth James King, for example, has sketched the process whereby the British foreign office exported industrial education on the Tuskegee model to the British colonies in Africa; while W. H. G. Armytage has explicated the influence of American ideals and examples on the English educational system itself. More recently, there have been the multifarious programs under national and international auspices in which everything from nursery schools to graduate medical education on the American model has been exported to countries around the world.[6]

[6] Kenneth James King, *Pan-Africanism and Education: A Study of Race, Philanthropy, and Education in the Southern States of America and East Africa* (Oxford: Clarendon Press, 1971); and W. H. G. Armytage, *The American Influence on English Education* (London: Routledge and Kegan Paul, 1967).

Finally, there was the export of large numbers of people who taught by example, by design, and by force—armies of travelers, armies of technicians, and armies of occupation. Metropolitan powers, as we have seen, teach variously but insistently; and the fact that in this particular instance the power doing the teaching was still in the process of defining itself—its own education still proffered a *paideia* in the making—in no way lessened the impact of that teaching. For, as Alexis de Tocqueville noted very early in the nation's history, a lack of self-definition is not at all incompatible with a garrulous patriotism; indeed, the one may well occasion the other. Americans have been far more concerned, historically, with Americanization than Canadians have been with Canadianization, and this may well stem from the fact that Canadians have been less preoccupied with self-definition. As a number of historians have made clear, whereas Americans have used the metaphor of the melting pot, Canadians have preferred to speak of the mosaic. [7]

Having stressed this shift in the balance of trade in products and ideas over the past hundred years, it is perhaps well to point out that the traffic was never unidirectional. America imported manual training from Russia, the kindergarten from Germany, impressionist painting from France, and rock music from England, and it then returned them to Europe in transformed American versions, along with indigenously developed junior high schools, abstractionist paintings, and jazz.

[7] Alexis de Tocqueville, *Democracy in America*, edited by Phillips Bradley (2 vols.; New York: Alfred A. Knopf, 1946), 1:241–245 and *passim;* and Allan Smith, "Metaphor and Nationality in North America," *The Canadian Historical Review*, 51 (1970): 247–275.

The point is important to emphasize: however discernibly American the traditions of American education have been at different times in history, they have never been exclusively American. Indeed, the very concept of an American education is problematical, and the definition must not be limited by failure to acknowledge the movement of ideas and institutions across geographical boundaries.

II

THE CHANGES in the institutions of American education during the century following 1876 were prodigious, and occasionally of revolutionary pace and proportion. The household continued to undergo the profound transformation associated with modernization, and the transformation continued to proceed variously in different regions and among different ethnic, religious, and social groups. The great immigrations of the forty years preceding World War I brought extended kin networks of urban Russian and Polish Jews and rural Lithuanian and Italian Catholics, who crowded into the cities of the Northeast, as well as networks of rural Scandinavian Lutherans and rural Greek and Armenian Eastern Orthodox, who went west to create the farms and work the mines of Minnesota, Montana, and the Dakotas. Each of these kin networks responded to the phenomenon of modernization differently, with some remaining traditionally extended, patriarchal, and coercive of women and children until well into the twentieth century. Yet there were certain more general trends that moved relentlessly forward. The median size of the American household shrank from 4.48 in 1890 to 3.40 in 1930 to approximately 3.0 in 1970, meaning that, though there were still very large and very small households and though many households of all sizes remained closely related to nearby kin, the average American household had fewer children and fewer adults (that is, fewer aunts, uncles, grandparents, and boarders). Furthermore, both the absolute number of divorces and the rate of divorce rose, meaning that even with a relatively high rate of remarriage there were more single-parent households. In addition, there was a growing participation of married women and, among them, mothers of school-age children, in the work force, particularly during and after World War II. Thus, whereas 26 percent of married women with children between the ages of six and seventeen were engaged in or seeking work in 1948, that figure had reached 51 percent by early 1974.

The church manifested a greater presence in American life, though paradoxically it seemed to exert less power. Church membership statistics are notoriously inaccurate, but there was a clear indication of growing affiliation on the part of the American people, with the proportion of the population reporting church membership rising from 35 percent in 1890 to 43 percent in 1920 to 55 percent in 1950 to a peak of 69 percent in 1960, after which there was a falling off to 62 percent in 1970. When the Bureau of the Census in 1957 asked a national sample of people over fourteen years of age, "What is your religion?" 96 percent indicated some religious preference, with seventy million listing it as Protestant, thirty million as Roman Catholic, four million as Jewish, and eleven million as "other," and 4 percent indicated no religious preference or no religion at all. Now, the problem, of course, is to determine what the increase in affiliation and the prevalence of religious identification actually meant with respect to the influence of the church as educator. I would judge that they implied the church's continuing effect on religiosity and on popular subscription to and profession of a generalized supernaturalism but not necessarily its continuing influence on behavior, as evidenced by a series of crises extending from the trial of John T. Scopes in 1925, to the repeal of prohibition in 1933, to the election of John F. Kennedy in 1960, to the use of contraceptive drugs and devices in the 1970s.

The schools, I believe, were transformed significantly, partly by the political prodding of a diverse group of publics, partly under the influence of progressive educational theory, and partly by the fact of their own increasing holding power—as time passed, they retained a growing proportion of the age group between five and seventeen (the proportion rose from 74 percent in 1910 to 87 percent in 1970). Vocational training was introduced as a principal component of the junior and senior high-school curriculum; social studies programs sought to connect the school's substance to local community activities; physical education and the arts made their way into the curriculum; a substantial extracurriculum developed, organized largely around student athletics, student journalism, student government, and student clubs; and the materials of study and instruction changed to reflect a greater concern for the individual child and his progress through the various academic subjects. In general, the school tried to do more things for more children and adults: it was a center for the antihookworm effort of the General Education Board in the South; it was a center for the vocational guidance program in the cities of the Northeast; and it was a center for the agricultural extension program in the hamlets and towns of the Midwest. All of this was made permanent in stone, so to speak, as the new school architecture of the 1930s incorporated assembly rooms, gymnasiums, swimming pools, playgrounds, laboratories, shops, kitchens, cafeterias, and infirmaries into buildings erected with WPA funds.

The colleges and universities also expanded and diversified their enrollments and offerings. In 1890, the total enrollment in American colleges and universities was 157 thousand, or 1.8 percent of the population between eighteen and twenty-four; in 1920, the enrollment was almost 600 thousand, or 4.7 percent of the population between eighteen and twenty-four; in 1950, the enrollment was 2.7 million, or 17 percent of the population between eighteen and twenty-four; and in 1970, the enrollment was 7.5 million, or 31 percent of the population between eighteen and twenty-four. These steadily increasing enrollments also diversified after 1890, along lines of class, sex, and race. Moreover, college and university students pursued a greater variety of subjects in a greater variety of institutions at a greater variety of levels. At the same time as undergraduate education became popularized, graduate and professional education proliferated to embrace more occupations and coalesced to form the comprehensive American universities of the twentieth century. Medicine, law, and theology came into their own, along with graduate training in the arts and sciences; but so did education, business, engineering, nursing, librarianship, social work, public administration, police science, and hotel management. And they coalesced, as Laurence R. Veysey has made abundantly clear, into a variety of different sorts of universities, ranging from Cornell, with its explicit commitment to utilitarianism, to Princeton, with its explicit commitment to liberal culture, to the University of Wisconsin, with its explicit commitment to social service. The booming, buzzing confusion that had resulted by the 1920s drew the mordant criticism of Abraham Flexner, who deplored the American emphasis on cash versus culture and on utility versus intellect. Later, during and after World War II, the confusion was organized into the federal-grant university by managers surely as expert in their own right as the "captains of erudition" that Thorstein Veblen had pilloried a half-century before.[8]

Some of the most profound changes occurred in the nature of the work situation as an educative setting. The factory, the mine, the office, the transportation system, the government bureau, and the human-service institution, which were still on the margins of a predominantly agricultural economy as late as the 1870s, moved to the center of the economic stage, and the farm too became an industry rather than an extension of the household. As a result, apprenticeship moved for the

[8] Laurence R. Veysey, *The Emergence of the American University* (Chicago: University of Chicago Press, 1965); Abraham Flexner, *Universities: American, English, German* (New York: Oxford University Press, 1930); and Thorstein Veblen, *The Higher Learning in America: A Memorandum on the Conduct of Universities by Business Men* (New York: B. W. Huebsch, 1918).

most part to the place of work, and indeed the characteristics and control of apprenticeship became a matter of considerable contention in early twentieth-century labor negotiations, with employers wanting to retain firm control over recruitment to and training for the trades and with unions wanting just as strongly to regulate them in the interest of advancing the welfare of the workers and preventing the encroachment of scabs. Very quickly, however, apprenticeship stopped being educative— that is, a systematic training in the elements of a craft or trade—and became exploitative—that is, an initial career stage in which the worker was paid very little for repetitive performance of an unskilled job. In the coal mines, it may have worked fairly effectively, since the principal demand of the job was brute strength and superhuman lungs; in factories, offices, and service institutions, exploitative apprenticeship was inefficient, with the result that industry began both to demand vocational preparation of the schools and colleges and to provide more and more vocational preparation of its own. One outcome of the latter was that by the 1950s companies like General Electric, the Radio Corporation of America, and Johnson & Johnson actually taught more advanced mathematics and science than did many universities—and this quite apart from the managerial programs they conducted for executives and the understudy training they provided for lower-rung supervisory personnel. Finally, the unions undertook training programs too, both in the substance and the skills of work itself and in matters relating to labor negotiation, such as parliamentary procedure and the law of collective bargaining.

The complex of rehabilitative and custodial institutions that began to develop during the pre–Civil War era also expanded, proliferated, and diffused across the nation. Beginning with Stanton Coit's organization of the Neighborhood Guild on New York's Lower East Side in 1886, the social settlement emerged across the country as a privately sponsored, quasi-public, social-service agency, committed to the development of new methods of alleviating the appalling effects of poverty. Out of the settlement came an array of institutional innovations, all of them involving education and rehabilitation in one way or another—the visiting nurse, the visiting teacher, the child guidance clinic, the child-care center, the community recreation center, and the senior citizens' center. Out of the social settlement, too, came a new educational profession, social work. Contemporaneously, the juvenile court and its appended apparatus of probation officers and reformatories won gradual acceptance across the country, while asylums, almshouses, and penitentiaries under public sponsorship became common.

Institutions for the development and diffusion of knowledge also multiplied. Museums, aquaria, botanical gardens, and specialized libraries served as elite centers of culture during the later nineteenth century, before the colleges had committed themselves to the production of knowledge as well as its distribution; later, during the twentieth century, such institutions forged links with the emerging universities or were actually annexed by them. At the same time, libraries, lyceums, chautauquas, fairs, expositions, and conventions burgeoned as agencies for sharing, diffusing, and displaying knowledge, art, and entertainment. Many, like the chautauquas, were both national and local; the styles of knowledge, art, and entertainment they presented were frequently common across state and regional lines, while the displays and performances themselves were local and immediate. Much the same might be said of the elaborate and immensely innovative system of agricultural extension and home-demonstration agents established under the Smith-Lever Act of 1914; they proffered knowledge, information, and skills that had been developed by the agricultural colleges, the agricultural experiment stations, and the Department of Agriculture and that were frequently common across state and regional lines, but their displays and their teaching were local and immediate—on demonstration farms, at agricultural and comprehensive high schools, at local and regional fairs, and at short courses at the various state universities.

Perhaps the most revolutionary educational development of the period after 1876 was the rise of the mass media of communication, the press, cinema, radio, and television. The number of newspapers peaked in 1914, with about twenty-five hundred dailies and almost fifteen thousand weeklies; the number of periodicals peaked in 1929, at over five thousand. Thereafter, the number of serials remained constant or declined, but circulation continued to increase, to a point where in 1940 there were nine thousand newspapers with a combined circulation of 96 million and five thousand periodicals with a combined circulation of 239 million. The technology of cinema was developed during the 1890s, with the first American "story" films (as opposed to "incident" films) dating from the early years of the twentieth century and the first sound films dating from the later 1920s. Thereafter, the average weekly attendance at films in the United States climbed from eighty million in 1929 to ninety million in 1930, then dipped during the Depression, returned to ninety million again after World War II, and then fell off in response to the advent of television. The technology of radio broadcasting was also developed during the 1890s, with the first commercial broadcast over KDKA in Pittsburgh in 1920. By the end of 1922, over five hundred stations had been licensed, and the decades thereafter saw a steady and rapid rise in the number of families owning one radio set or more, to the point of saturation. Finally, the technology of television broadcasting was evolved during the 1930s, but the commercial development of television did not begin in earnest until after World War II, when it spread through the United States more rapidly than any other major technological innovation in history: in 1950, fewer than 5 percent of American households had television sets; by 1975, the figure had leveled off at around 96 percent, with some households reporting two or more receivers. Now, the mass media claimed to provide information and entertainment, leaving "education" to the schools; but the fact is that they educated relentlessly, precisely as they informed, entertained, hawked products, and sold services. As early as 1922 in *Public Opinion*, Walter Lippmann called attention to the educational phenomenon of simultaneously creating the same "pictures" in the minds of millions of people and pointed to the profound bearing of that phenomenon on politics and public affairs.

Finally, there was the conscript army, not usually seen as an educative agency but profoundly educative by virtue of its varied composition and character. Bringing together millions of men and women from all regions and walks of life in newly assigned roles and statuses, the conscript army also educated relentlessly—through apprenticeship, on-site instruction, self-teaching manuals, formal schooling, and direct example. It proffered models of behavior, models of speech, models of valuing and believing, and modes of thinking and analysis. And, while its immediate and explicit business was the art of war, it taught many other things as well, among them, ironically enough, behaviors and outlooks that could liberate individuals from parochial preoccupations and aspirations.

Once again, it is the ways in which these institutions affected one another politically and pedagogically, and related to one another in configurations of education, that I should like to dwell upon. One can reiterate the point about diversity and one can repeat the caveats about the excluded. And yet, inasmuch as some elements of education became increasingly national during the late nineteenth and early twentieth centuries, their effects became increasingly nationwide. An instrument like the Stanford-Binet test of intelligence, a series of textbooks like the Macmillan basal readers, a film like *Gone with the Wind*, and an institution like the army during World War I and World War II—these were national educative influences that transcended the bounds of locality. But they were not necessarily federal influences, and this is an important distinction to emphasize. The army was, of course, a federal influence, and so was the vocational training program inaugurated by the Smith-Hughes Act of 1917; so also was the

WPA cultural program of the 1930s, with its "people's theatre," its writers' projects, its community art centers, its research into the folk music of the Appalachians, and its general commitment to "arts for the millions." But there was far more of national scope than the federal government sponsored, all of which made Americans subject to a greater commonality of educative influences than at any previous time in their history.

The configuration of education that touched most people came to include household, church, school, work, and mass communications, including serial publications and later films and radio and television broadcasts. The colleges and the institutions of rehabilitation also affected growing numbers of individuals, as did libraries, museums, cultural and entertainment agencies of one sort or another, and a plethora of voluntary associations. One sees the configuration clearly in the Lynds' study of Muncie, Indiana, during the mid-1920s. An industrial city of some thirty-five thousand situated between Fort Wayne and Indianapolis, Muncie was a center of bottle and jar production, tool- and diemaking, and automotive parts manufacture. In their six classic sections on getting a living, making a home, training the young, using leisure, engaging in religious practices, and engaging in community activities, the Lynds provided a remarkable map of Muncie as a configuration of education. Muncie's families were getting smaller, having shrunk from an average size of 4.6 in 1890 to 3.8 in 1920, the decrease owing to the presence of fewer children and fewer dependent adults in each household. In addition, more and more mothers, especially working-class mothers, were going to work, and more and more children were caught up in a round of activities with agemates that took them out of their homes three, four, five, six, and seven evenings a week. Church membership and church attendance remained common, with the total weekly attendance at all church services (the figure included duplications) averaging twenty-one thousand—incidentally, almost a third of all the adult clubs in Muncie were church-related. The schools were already showing the influence of the progressive education movement, particularly in their concern for vocational guidance and vocational education in the high school and in the considerable expansion of the extracurriculum, with its plethora of social and athletic activities. Muncie boasted a college too, founded in 1918, and by the 1920s the city was also sending growing numbers of students to the state university in Bloomington. [9]

The Lynds began their study with a chapter entitled "The Dominance of Getting a Living," pointing to the fact that forty-three out of every hundred people in Muncie (80 percent of them male) specialized day after day in going to work and earning a living. By the 1920s most of these people were working outside the home, in factories, shops, or offices. As for mass communications, newspapers circulated briskly in Muncie: eighty-nine hundred of the city's ninety-two hundred homes received the morning paper, sixty-seven hundred received the afternoon paper, and some twelve to fifteen hundred copies of out-of-town newspapers were sold daily, including eight copies of *The New York Times*. Radio, interestingly enough, had not yet taken hold: in a 1924 count of

[9] Robert S. Lynd and Helen Merrell Lynd, *Middletown: A Study in American Culture* (New York: Harcourt, Brace and Company, 1929) and *Middletown in Transition: A Study in Cultural Conflicts* (New York: Harcourt, Brace and Company, 1937).

representative neighborhoods, only 12 percent of the business-class homes and 6 percent of the working-class homes were found to have radios. Finally, Muncie had a children's court and a county poor asylum, the latter a catchall for the insane, the handicapped, the shiftless, and the so-called respectable homeless. Muncie had a public library, from which there were almost a hundred thousand loans annually. And Muncie boasted almost five hundred clubs, with a total membership of well over twenty-five thousand (once again, including duplications).

Beyond this sketch of the pattern itself, there is much in the Lynds' analysis that illuminates the relationships among the several institutions: the extensive influence of the so-called X-family through the several components of the configuration, the differential use of various components of the configuration by the working class as contrasted with the business class, the far-reaching effect of the churches, and the profound transformations already being wrought by the automobile, the motion picture, and the radio. Indeed, in one of their most telling observations, the Lynds noted: "At no point is one brought up more sharply against the impossibility of studying Middletown as a self-contained, self-starting community than as one watches the space-binding leisure-time inventions imported from without—automobile, motion picture, and radio—reshaping the city." If the configurations of American education had already begun to transcend the bounds of the locality in the nineteenth century, that tendency was becoming even more pronounced in the twentieth.[10]

[10] Lynd and Lynd, *Middletown*, p. 271.

Leaving the example of Muncie, and begging the question of how representative the city really was, I would remark several other changes in the relationships among educative institutions. First, as the household declined in size and influence, the school increased in holding power and effect. And the school's new potency was both direct and indirect. On the one hand, children spent more time with their teachers and were doubtless more profoundly influenced by them, though there is no one-to-one relationship between time spent and influence exerted, or indeed between intended influence and actual outcome. On the other hand, children, and particularly adolescents, also spent more time with one another, creating a newly powerful element in their education, namely, the peer group. Children had always had friends, to be sure; but now there was a discernible age-structured group that gathered daily in a particular institution, the school. Moreover, that group became the target of special films, special radio programs, and special advertising campaigns for special products; put otherwise, that group became a special market clientele, which was systematically taught styles of dress, entertainment, and food, or, more generally, special styles of consumption. The household mediated this educative influence to some extent, but the influence was powerful nonetheless and in many ways competed with the purposeful efforts of parents, pastors, and schoolteachers.

Second, the school increasingly mediated work experience. Inasmuch as the high school assumed responsibility for vocational guidance and vocational education, it increasingly directed students, especially male students, to particular kinds of jobs or to a continuing education in college, which itself directed students to particular kinds of jobs (the nondirection of female students was, of course, simply another aspect of the same process). Decisions that had formerly been made largely within the household or by the individual in isolation were now made within a new setting, the school, in collaboration with a new professional, the guidance counselor. The shift was also reciprocal, in that business became more and more interested in schools as agencies for recruiting and training workers for industry, and indeed business came to think of such training as a "return" on the taxes paid for education. The relationship became formalized in the phenomenon of credentialing, as school, college, and university preparation became a surrogate for less formal modes of training on the one hand and more direct demonstrations of competence on the other.

Third, as the average work week decreased from sixty hours or more in the 1870s to some forty hours in the 1940s and 1950s, people had more time to pursue leisure activities, including self-education, mutual education, formal and informal instruction, and entertainment with educational significance. Listening to the radio; reading newspapers, magazines, and books; going to the movies; participating in clubs and other voluntary associations; visiting museums, concert halls, and theaters; enrolling in adult education courses, traveling by automobile to national parks—all became more possible. And, as the possibility increased, more opportunities came into being—more newspapers, magazines, and books, more films, more libraries, more clubs, more schools of every variety, more museums, concert halls, and theaters, and more national parks. Of course, people also took second jobs, repainted their houses, slept more, or simply wasted time. Surely nothing here is meant to imply that leisure suddenly unleashed a frenzy of teaching and learning.

Fourth, there were particular educative agencies that were central in the export of American culture overseas—the church, the corporation, the mass medium of communication, and the army. Each offered a partial version of American life, the missionary being no more representative than the salesman, the soldier, or, most intriguing perhaps, the hero in the grade-B western. What is important to bear in mind, however, is that the partiality of the version bore no relation to its power; and the fact is that people in many countries of the world assumed that the grade-B western truly represented the values, the qualities, and the diurnal round of activities of ordinary American life.

As before, I should point out that these generalizations applied differently in different communities and in different segments of the same community, and that it is therefore necessary to look at particular instances to see them operationally. A brief glance at New York City, perhaps the quintessential metropolitan community of twentieth-century America, will serve as an illustration, though, again, it is not my intention to picture New York as typical or representative. The city began an explosive growth of population in the 1790s, which continued until the leveling off of the 1940s and 1950s. The population was 3.4 million in 1900, two years after the consolidation of the five boroughs into Greater New York; that figure rose to 5.6 million in 1920 and leveled off at just under 8 million in

1950, where it remained for the next twenty years. In 1900, 84 percent of the white heads of families in the city were either themselves foreign-born or the children of immigrants; in 1940, that figure was still as high as 64 percent. The origins of the foreign-born population were exceedingly varied, with the principal concentrations having come from Italy, Russia, Ireland, Germany, Poland, Austria, and Great Britain. In addition, there was a large black population, primarily but not wholly native-born, which increased from 61,000 in 1900 to 459,000 in 1940 to 1,668,000 in 1970, and a substantial population of Puerto Rican birth, which increased from 61,000 in 1940 to 430,000 in 1960. Predictably, household education was extraordinarily diverse in New York City, with respect to everything from language and values to relationships with neighbors and kin. Predictably, too, churches and synagogues were also diverse: a fairly reliable 1952 survey indicated that New Yorkers reported themselves as 47.6 percent Catholic, 26.4 percent Jewish, and 22.8 percent Protestant; but these figures must be further refined within the several categories: there were Gregorian Catholics, Italian Catholics, and Irish Catholics; Reformed Jews and ultraorthodox Jews; Episcopalian as well as Pentecostal Protestants.

Given its demographic base and institutional specialization, nineteenth-century New York had already developed a complex educational configuration, which included not only the household, the church, the school, the college, the newspaper, and the factory, but also rehabilitative, recreational, and cultural agencies of every sort and variety. During the twentieth century, every component of the configuration became larger, more intricate, and more specialized. Enrollments in the public-school system rose from 420,000 in 1900 to 1,113,000 in 1930, and then declined to 987,000 in 1960; but it is important to recognize that the gross enrollment figures covered a wide range of schools—not only elementary schools, junior high schools, and comprehensive senior high schools, but also specialized academic and vocational schools of music, the performing arts, food trades, aviation trades, needle trades, and the like, special schools for difficult children, delinquent children, and deaf children, and a variety of part-time continuation schools. Alongside the public-school system were several substantial parochial school systems, a large number of independent schools, and a mind-boggling range of special entrepreneurial schools that taught everything from dancing to diamond-cutting to foreign languages to radio repair.

The same range and diversity marked the higher education system. By 1937, when Queens College was founded, there were four city colleges offering tuition-free undergraduate education. In addition, there were the two older independent universities, Columbia University and New York University, several church-related institutions such as Fordham University and Yeshiva College, and a number of specialized institutions such as Finch College, Parsons School of Design, the Juilliard School of Music, and the Rockefeller Institute. Beyond these, and in many cases closely related to them, there were by the 1930s more than a dozen art museums, a score of historical museums, five science museums, and a half-dozen botanical gardens or zoological institutes. There was a collection of libraries that included the New York Public Library, with its main reference department and its threescore local circulation branches and subbranches, and a fascinating sprinkling of independent libraries, ranging from the Grolier Club Library to the library of the American Numismatic Society. And then there were the networks of concert halls, theaters, and art galleries, which displayed the artistic products of a national and international cultural capital.

New York's rehabilitative and custodial system included, in addition to the domestic relations court and its network of probation officers and social-service workers, a potpourri of public, quasi-public, independent, and church-related institutions—jails and reformatories, orphan asylums and settlement houses, child guidance clinics and municipal shelters, custodial facilities euphemistically known as training schools, and almshouses euphemistically known as hospitals. In 1939 the city's *Directory of Social Agencies* listed some eight hundred institutions and organizations operating in the fields of health, family service, recreation, vocational guidance, and custodial and correctional supervision, of which roughly a hundred were departments of government; and they oversaw everything from the care of foundlings to the care of the aged. [11]

In the realm of mass communications, New York boasted eight daily newspapers, some of them such as the *Times*, the *Tribune*, and the *Daily Worker* having national and international circulations, thirty-five foreign language dailies, and three Negro weeklies. The city also housed fourteen radio stations, all of which could be heard within the metropolitan area

[11] [New York City] Welfare Council, *Directory of Social Agencies*, 1939–40 (New York: Columbia University Press, 1939).

and many of which could be heard elsewhere (it was also the headquarters of the National Broadcasting Company and the Columbia Broadcasting System networks). And, as a center of publishing, New York sent forth a profusion of books, magazines, and other printed matter for mass and specialized consumption.

One must add to these a vast range of social and cultural clubs, associations, and organizations, an infinite variety of crafts, businesses, services, and industries, and the countless comings and goings of individuals and groups from every corner of the nation and the world for purposes of commerce, convention, and tourism, to gain a true sense of the complexity of the city during the 1930s as originator, as importer and exporter, and as mediator of culture, in sum, as a center of education.

At least one additional point should be made. During the 1930s, when the Lynds prepared *Middletown in Transition*, Muncie, Indiana, was of a size that any particular citizen could grasp, conceive, and even comprehend the whole. During the same period, when Lou Gody and his colleagues on the Federal Writers' Project published *The New York City Guide*, New York City was of a size that virtually no one could grasp, conceive, or comprehend the whole. There were more Italians in New York City than in Rome, more Irish than in Dublin, more blacks than in any African city, and more Jews than in any other city of the world. For all intents and purposes, a person experienced New York through one or another of its neighborhoods or its ethnic or religious communities: one experienced the city via the Lower East Side, or Brownsville, or Yorkville, or Harlem, or Riverdale. And this fact had profound implications for the configurations of New York City education. Even in eighteenth-century Dedham, one could live one's early years within a cluster of white families dominated by a revivalist pastor and only later enter into significant association with other sorts of children and adults in a district school. And indeed in nineteenth-century Macoupin County, one could live to adulthood largely within the confines of a world bounded by Lutheran households, a Lutheran church, and a Lutheran school. And neither eighteenth-century Dedham nor nineteenth-century Macoupin was isolated or insulated: they were both in continuing communication with external cultural and religious institutions committed to education. In twentieth-century New York, however, both the power of what we might call the subconfigurations of education and the range and extent of the external influences had increased. One could grow up on the Lower East Side within a network of institutions that was referred to as the New York Kehillah (the Hebrew word "kehillah" means "community") and have little to do with the outside world until going to the public library, or taking a job, or being drafted into the army; and if one didn't go to the library, or worked in an all-Jewish factory, or managed to avoid military service, one could live one's entire life in the kehillah, aware of external influences only as intrusions. Similarly, one could grow up in Harlem, after it had become predominantly black in the 1920s and 1930s, within a network of black private and public institutions and have little to do with the outside world, once again, until voluntarily venturing forth or going to work or joining the military. And, indeed, in a society that practiced racial segregation, venturing forth to the wrong place in the wrong way was discouraged by a variety of means that ranged from subtle warnings to violent exclusion. As a result, the Lower East Side Jew and the Harlem black could come of age in a leading metropolis of the twentieth century within fairly confined configurations of household, synagogue or church, school, and peer group, and could simultaneously hear radio broadcasts that originated in California or Canada. Moreover, this very metropolis was at the same time exporting national styles of clothing to the rest of America and American styles of painting and architecture to the rest of the world.[12]

Which educational biographies might illustrate the dynamics of education in twentieth-century New York? The philosopher Morris Raphael Cohen was born in Russian Poland in 1880, was educated by family and kin, notably his grandfather, by a European *cheder*, and by the synagogue until he came to the United States and settled on the Lower East Side in 1892. Thereafter, he received his education from the local public schools, from the Aguilar Free Library at the Educational Alliance, from the Yiddish Socialist daily *Arbeiter Zeitung*, from the College of the City of New York and Harvard University, and from the full range of literary and political activities associated with the Socialist Labor Party. The painter Jacob Lawrence was born in Atlantic City in 1917, was educated in household, school, and church there and in Philadelphia, and was brought to Harlem as a teenager. He partici-

[12] Federal Writers' Project, Works Progress Administration, *New York City Guide* (1939; reprint ed.; New York: Octagon Books, 1970).

pated in recreational arts-and-crafts activities at Utopia House, attended art classes first at the 135th Street Public Library and then at a WPA project called the Harlem Art Workshop (while attending regular classes at the High School of Commerce), did a tour at the CCC camp in Middletown, New York, completed his formal studies at the American Artists School back in the city, and then joined the WPA Federal Arts Project, where he finished his Frederick Douglass cycle and began his Harriet Tubman cycle. Interestingly, Lawrence spent World War II as a member of the United States Coast Guard and had the good fortune to serve under a commanding officer who encouraged him to continue his painting and who was instrumental in having him assigned to the first "integrated" ship in the navy, the U.S.S. *Sea Cloud*, which Lawrence referred to as "the best democracy I've ever known." [13]

Perhaps it should be pointed out that at precisely the time that Cohen and Lawrence were successfully negotiating the educational configurations of the Lower East Side and Harlem for their own purposes, others were negotiating the same configurations quite differently but equally successfully. Alfred E. Smith, for example, who was seven years older than Morris Cohen, was born on the Lower East Side, the son of an Irish Catholic truck driver. The leading educational influences in his life were, first, a devoutly religious household collaborating with an active parish church, an active parish school, and an active parish youth group and, then, from the age of

[13] Morris Raphael Cohen, A *Dreamer's Journey* (Boston: The Beacon Press, 1949); and Milton W. Brown, *Jacob Lawrence* (New York: Whitney Museum of American Art, 1974), p. 13 and *passim*.

fourteen on, a succession of jobs that seem to have taught him how to get on with co-workers at the same time that he fulfilled the expectations of superiors. Smith recounted in his autobiography a rather prissy exchange in the 1911 session of the New York State Legislature, in which several speakers referred to themselves seriatim as "a Yale man," "a Harvard man," and "a U of M man," at which point Smith referred to himself as "an FFM man," FFM meaning Fulton Fish Market, otherwise known as the school of hard knocks. [14]

A quite different Smith, named Wilbur, who was six years older than Jacob Lawrence, was born in Harlem Hospital and actually grew up within sight of that institution. The chief educative influences in his life were also a strict working-class household (Wilbur Smith's father was a porter, and his mother a domestic), a nearby church with an extensive Sunday program, the public schools, and a succession of part-time jobs in local retail establishments. Smith entered the postal service shortly after dropping out of high school, via a civil service examination for which his schooling presumably helped to prepare him. He remained with the post office for the rest of his career. "If I had my life to live over again," he told an interviewer in 1974, "I would prefer to live it the same way I came up." [15]

[14] Alfred E. Smith, *Up to Now: An Autobiography* (New York: The Viking Press, 1929), pp. 111–112. See also Oscar Handlin, *Al Smith and His America* (Boston: Little, Brown and Company, 1958) and Richard O'Connor, *The First Hurrah: A Biography of Alfred E. Smith* (New York: G. P. Putnam's Sons, 1970).

[15] I am grateful to Dean Morse of the Conservation of Human Resources Project at Columbia University for the information on Wilbur Smith, which is taken from unpublished data he gathered in connection with a forthcoming book tentatively titled *Pride Against Prejudice.*

There were, of course, numerous contemporaries of Cohen, Lawrence, and the Smiths who negotiated the educational configurations of their time less successfully, failing to accomplish their own significant goals or indeed failing to develop any significant goals in the first place. Their biographies are ephemeral and less detailed, but profoundly poignant; their movement through New York's educational configurations can be traced in the stark proceedings of the children's court and the records of probation officers—latchkey children of broken families on home relief or private charity, with records of failure at school, truancy, and time spent in reformatories, followed by lives of alienating work and chronic despair.

What we know about the ways in which people interact with educational configurations indicates that the education of the home is often decisive and that educative styles first learned in the family hold much of the key to the patterns by which individuals engage in, move through, and combine educational experiences over a lifetime. Benjamin Franklin's *Autobiography* taught Americans that the road to success is paved in great measure by inventiveness, imaginativeness, and, above all, agency in negotiating the educational configurations of one's time; it did not trouble to mention that inventiveness, imaginativeness, and agency are not transmitted genetically but are themselves learned in what Poor Richard would have referred to as the school of experience. The point of the educational biography is to indicate the tremendous range and complexity of educational experience, not to trumpet the triumph of the self-made American.

III

RUSH WELTER once characterized the governmental policy of Jacksonian America as "anarchy with a schoolmaster," whereby he alluded to the apparent anomaly of laissez-faire liberals embracing public education. We know, of course, from Welter's own work that the Whigs who promoted public schooling and public rehabilitation institutions during the mid-nineteenth century were the same Whigs who advocated government assistance to entrepreneurial economic development via direct subsidies, internal improvements, and generally favorable treatment—in other words, it was less than anarchy and more than a schoolmaster. We also know that the disestablished churches of the 1830s and 1840s were actually working at many of the public tasks the liberals would later assign to the public schools. But Welter did point accurately to the significance of the great nineteenth-century shift in which the institutions of schooling and rehabilitation became the chief educational instruments of public policy and political development.[16]

That tendency became more pronounced during the twentieth century, as Americans placed broader and heavier responsibilities on public schools, public prisons, public reformatories, public child guidance clinics, and the like. The burden of the progressive movement in education and the social services consisted in more direct and more fundamental

[16] Rush Welter, *Popular Education and Democratic Thought in America* (New York: Columbia University Press, 1962), pp. 43, 50.

intervention in the education of more and more Americans, in the interest of equalizing opportunity and encouraging individual development and at the same time achieving a certain measure of socialization for public ends. The progressives argued, on the personal side, that everyone deserved a chance if human dignity were to mean anything and, on the social side, that the polity would benefit from the maximum development of human potential. Now, quite apart from the radical charge that all this was merely a rhetorical guise for massive coercion of the population to the dehumanizing requirements of a capitalist society—the socialist societies, incidentally, do not seem to be behaving very differently on the institutional side—the ironies have been profound and troubling. The schools did extend opportunity to many whose familial education had been impoverished and constraining, and they extended even more opportunity to many whose familial education had been rich and liberating; but such opportunity as they did extend was clearly inadequate for many individuals in both categories. In part, schoolpeople did not know enough; in part, they did not care enough; and in part, when they did know enough and care enough, they seemed unable to persuade the public to commit enough resources over sufficient periods of time. The same was true of the rehabilitative institutions, which were assigned the more difficult educational tasks and which were provided with even less adequate funds. In the absence of sufficient knowledge, sufficient care, and sufficient funds, schools and rehabilitative institutions alike too often ended up performing minimal custodial functions. In my opinion, the experience of the late 1960s demonstrated that a massive increment in public funds could provide more knowledge, more committed personnel, and more resources in sufficient quantities to begin to make a discernible difference in the direction of progressive aspirations; but the effort was halted too soon and for all the wrong reasons.

Granted this, two additional points should be made. First, the policies developed for public education at the local, state, and federal levels during the twentieth century—by which I mean policies for public schooling, public libraries, public rehabilitative institutions, and public broadcasting—have seldom been integral or comprehensive. The schools have been in one political and professional system, the libraries in another, the public rehabilitative institutions in another, and the public broadcasting institutions in still another. Separate professional faculties have dealt with the several institutions and their needs in the universities; and separate agencies, administrative authorities, and legislative committees have dealt with the institutions and their needs in the political arena. The disjunctions have been most apparent when educational problems have been viewed from the perspective of the client, as in the 1930s, when the New Deal tried to develop comprehensive youth policies, and in the 1960s and 1970s, when successive administrations in Washington have tried to develop comprehensive child-care policies.

Second, and far more fundamental, the educational history of the past few decades indicates that Americans may need to reconsider where to place the burden of their effort in education and how. Given the crucial importance of early nurture, the trends with respect to family size, composition, and stability since World War II, and in particular the movement of mothers into productive work outside the home, literally demand the formulation of comprehensive public policies regarding the care and education of young children. Given the pervasiveness of radio and television in the lives of the vast majority of Americans, and the relentless education provided by radio and television broadcasting, a fundamental rethinking of the traditional modes of support, licensing, and regulation is required in that realm. As the then Secretary of Commerce Herbert Hoover remarked during the early days of commercial radio during the 1920s, "It is inconceivable that we should allow so great a possibility for service to be drowned in advertising chatter." Given the significance of work in the lives of most Americans and the decisive education provided by work itself, an equally fundamental rethinking is required in connection with such matters as education for work, the educational dimensions of work, and the education needed as individuals develop within particular work settings or shift from one work setting to another. And, given the significance of leisure in the lives of most Americans and the education made possible by leisure, a fundamental reassessment is required in that domain as well. The point is not that schools, libraries, and traditional rehabilitative institutions have suddenly become unimportant; it is rather that the educational situation has undergone revolutionary changes, which demand that the public reconsider where it will invest its effort and in what measure and to what ends.[17]

[17] *The Memoirs of Herbert Hoover* (3 vols.; New York: The Macmillan Company, 1951–52), 2:140.

IV

MY ARGUMENT in these lectures has been for renewed attention to context, complexity, and relationship in our discussions of education, past, present, and future. Contrary to the drift of a good deal of scholarly opinion during the past ten years, I happen to believe that on balance the American education system has contributed significantly to the advancement of liberty, equality, and fraternity, in that complementarity and tension that mark the relations among them in a free society. I have reached that belief on the basis of evidence that is admittedly mixed and with a willingness to grant major imperfections in performance. The institutions of American education are human institutions: they have been guilty of their full share of evil, venality, and failure, and my phrase "on balance" is intended to take account of that fact. But it is also intended to convey my sense that the aspirations of American education have been more noble than base, and that its performance over the past two centuries has been more liberating of a greater diversity of human energies and potentialities than has been the case in most other eras and in most other places. As a historian, I believe it is important to make judgments, but I also believe that the judgments should be of this world and not some other.

However that may be, my judgment in this matter is less important than the fundamental fact of complexity. I do not mean to suggest that the educational situation is so complicated and intractable that nothing should be done until we learn more. I mean rather to urge that we go beyond studies that analyze the family or the church or the school or television in isolation and then pronounce on their educational effects, and beyond studies that scrutinize people through a single lens of class or race or religion or ethnicity and, once again, pronounce on educational outcomes. Individual institutions and individual variables are important, to be sure; but it is the ways in which they pattern themselves and relate to one another that give them their educational significance, and the ways in which their outcomes confirm, complement, or contradict one another that determine their educational effects. In sum, complexity has marked American education from the beginning, and I would hope for a renewed appreciation of the inescapable fact of complexity in our discussions of educational theory and policy during the years immediately ahead.

A NOTE ON

PROBLEMATICS AND

SOURCES

TWO DISCERNIBLE revisionist thrusts have marked the historiography of American education during the past twenty years. The first, beginning with Bernard Bailyn's *Education in the Forming of American Society* (Chapel Hill: University of North Carolina Press, 1960) and continuing down through the present work, has sought to locate the history of education more effectively within the context of general American history, on the one hand broadening the definition of education to include institutions other than schools and colleges and on the other hand broadening the questions asked and the problems considered to include the impact of education on the society that sustains it. The second, beginning with Michael Katz's *The Irony of Early School Reform* (Cambridge, Mass.: Harvard University Press, 1968) and continuing down through the most recent publications of Walter Feinberg, Samuel Bowles, and Herbert Gintis, has attempted to alter the political-economic consciousness brought to bear on the history of education, stressing the gulf between rhetoric and reality in the development of American education and pointing to the flawed values inherent in the rhetoric itself.

Both thrusts have precursors in the earlier literature, the former in such works as Samuel Eliot Morison's *The Puritan Pronaos* (New York: New York University Press, 1935) or Clement Eaton's *Freedom of Thought in the Old South* (Durham, N.C.: Duke University Press, 1940), the latter in such works as Merle Curti's *The Social Ideas of American Educators* (New York: Charles Scribner's Sons, 1935) or Sidney L. Jackson's *America's Struggle for Free Schools* (Washington, D.C.: American Council on Public Affairs, 1941). Both thrusts are Whiggish insofar as they are policy-oriented, though each is at the same time anti-Whiggish in its own particular way, the former seeking to avoid presentism through more explicit attention to historical context, the latter seeking to avoid self-congratulation through a more radical criticism of the past. Both thrusts have reached out to the behavioral sciences for their explanatory concepts, and both have drawn significantly on such recent methodological innovations as family reconstitution, prosopography, and historical demography. And both have attempted to be more systematic and precise in seeking to determine the outcomes of education.

Yet, that said, the two thrusts have contributed very differently to the problematics of the history of education, to the nature of the questions asked and the character of the answers proffered. The former has been essentially latitudinarian, directing its attention to the full range of institutions that educate, to the changing relationships among those institutions, and to the various ways in which particular individuals and groups have experienced those institutions at different times in American history. The latter, for all its political radicalism, has been academically conservative, concentrating almost exclusively on the management, substance, and effects of schooling; in fact, the only significant departure from an overweaning preoccupation with schooling is Michael Katz's illuminating chapter on the Massachusetts state reform school in *The Irony of Early School Reform*, a subject to which Katz has never returned.

A number of recent review articles have attempted to assess the development of the field since the middle 1950s, the best of which is Douglas Sloan, "Historiography and the History of Education," in Fred Kerlinger, ed., *Review of Research in Education*, 1 (1973): 239–269. Sloan's commentary interweaves the two thrusts I have described, devoting lengthy sections, seriatim, to historiographical cross-fertilization, demythologizing the history of schools, education and the "rest of society," and education and enculturation. In addition, Sloan comments incisively on the academic conservatism of the so-called radical revisionists, observing their tendency to remain within the confines of an older schoolbound historiography at the same time as they substitute a theory of the progressive degeneration of public schooling for the more traditional (though equally simplistic) theory of its progressive evolution. Beyond the historiographical work per se, there is Michael B.

Katz, ed., *Education in American History: Readings on the Social Issues* (New York: Praeger Publishers, 1973), an anthology designed to present the new historiography in a form suitable for beginning students. And then there is Geraldine Jonçich Clifford's survey for a forthcoming volume of the *Review of Research in Education*, which builds on the Sloan essay and carries the historiographical account through 1975.

My effort here will be to review the work of the past twenty years with the question of a new problematics for the history of American education uppermost in mind. In so doing, I shall make only passing reference to ideological issues, and I shall refer only occasionally to the work on European, African, and Asian education, and then only as it illuminates the problematics of the American material. And I shall make no attempt to be exhaustive, preferring to cite exemplary studies rather than to survey the literature in its entirety.

II

I HAVE DEFINED education as the deliberate, systematic, and sustained effort to transmit, evoke, or acquire knowledge, attitudes, values, skills, or sensibilities, as well as any outcomes of that effort. The definition stresses intentionality, though I am well aware that learning takes place in many situations where intentionality is not present. It makes room for study as well as instruction, thereby embracing the crucial realm of self-education. And it acknowledges that behavior, preferences, and tastes are involved, as well as knowledge and understanding. It sees education as a process more limited than what the sociologist would call socialization or the anthropologist enculturation, though obviously inclusive of many of the same phenomena. And it recognizes that there is often a conflict between what educators are trying to teach and what is learned from the ordinary business of living.

The definition is latitudinarian in at least two major respects. First, it permits us several angles of vision with regard to the interplay of generations. Education may be viewed as intergenerational, with adults teaching children (recall Bernard Bailyn's definition of education in *Education in the Forming of American Society* [p. 14] as "the entire process by which culture transmits itself across the generations") or with children teaching adults (recall Oscar Handlin's poignant remarks in *The Uprooted* [2nd ed.; Boston: Little, Brown and Company, 1973, chap. 9] concerning the mediative role of second-generation immigrants in interpreting the culture of the new society to their parents and grandparents—"the young wore their nativity like a badge that marked their superiority over their immigrant elders"); it may be viewed as intragenerational (recall Robert F. Berkhofer's account of Protestant missions to the American Indians in *Salvation and the Savage: An Analysis of Protestant Missions and American Indian Response, 1787–1862* [Lexington: University of Kentucky Press, 1965], which makes such apt use of the concept of acculturation); or it may be viewed as a self-conscious coming of age (recall Joan Dash's sensitive biography of Maria Goeppert-Mayer in *A Life of One's Own: Three Gifted Women and the Men They Married* [New York: Harper & Row, 1973]).

135

Second, the definition projects us beyond the schools and colleges to the multiplicity of individuals and institutions that educate—parents, peers, siblings, and friends, as well as families, churches, synagogues, libraries, museums, summer camps, benevolent societies, agricultural fairs, settlement houses, factories, publishers, radio stations, and television networks. It alerts us to the numerous occupational groups (only some of which have been professionalized) associated with educational institutions, and it directs our attention to the variety of pedagogies they employ.

With these comments in mind, perhaps the first assertion that might be made about a new problematics for the history of education is that it must deal with a broad range of educational associations and institutions and the diverse interrelationships between each of these associations and institutions and the social systems that maintain them and are in turn affected by them. In studying these, the historian will inevitably draw upon a much wider variety of literatures than has traditionally been the case. With respect to schools and colleges, for instance, one thinks immediately of Carl F. Kaestle, *The Evolution of an Urban School System: New York City, 1750–1850* (Cambridge, Mass.: Harvard University Press, 1974), Laurence R. Veysey, *The Emergence of the American University* (Chicago: University of Chicago Press, 1974), John S. Whitehead, *The Separation of College and State: Columbia, Dartmouth, Harvard, and Yale, 1776–1876* (New Haven: Yale University Press, 1973), and Patricia Albjerg Graham, *Community & Class in American Education, 1865–1918* (New York: John Wiley & Sons, 1974); but one might also refer to the chapters on the schools in Laurence Veysey, *The Communal Experience: Anarchists and Mystical Counter-Cultures in America* (New York: Harper & Row, 1973) and to the sections on the universities in Howard S. Miller, *Dollars for Research: Science and Its Patrons in Nineteenth-Century America* (Seattle: University of Washington Press, 1970). With respect to the family, one thinks, *inter alia,* of John Demos, *A Little Commonwealth: Family Life in Plymouth Colony* (New York: Oxford University Press, 1970) and Bernard Farber, *Guardians of Virtue: Salem Families in 1800* (New York: Basic Books, 1972). With respect to the church, monographs as different as Sidney E. Mead, *The Lively Experiment: The Shaping of Christianity in America* (New York: Harper & Row, 1963) and David D. Hall, *The Faithful Shepherd: A History of the New England Ministry in the Seventeenth Century* (Chapel Hill: University of North Carolina Press, 1972) come to mind as studies that deal extensively with education, even though their authors clearly had other agenda in mind. With respect to the social settlement, Allen F. Davis, *Spearheads of Reform: The Social Settlements and the Progressive Movement, 1890–1914* (New York: Oxford University Press, 1967) is the most suggestive work. With respect to rehabilitative institutions, David J. Rothman, *The Discovery of the Asylum: Social Order and Disorder in the New Republic* (Boston: Little, Brown and Company, 1971) is similarly paradigmatic, whether or not one accepts Rothman's particular arguments. With respect to book publishers, Eugene Exman, *The Brothers Harper* (New York: Harper & Row, 1965) is exemplary, while on newspapers and magazines, Frank Luther Mott, *American*

Journalism: A History of Newspapers in the United States Through 260 Years, 1690 to 1950 (New York: The Macmillan Company, 1950) and *A History of American Magazines* (5 vols.; Cambridge, Mass.: Harvard University Press, 1930–1968) remain definitive. For radio and television, Erik Barnouw, *A History of Broadcasting in the United States* (3 vols.; New York: Oxford University Press, 1966–1970) is the central work.

Along with these various literatures dealing with the several institutions that educate, the historian of education will also be interested in the biographies of men and women who have spent their lives teaching in those institutions. Thus, there will be useful material not only in such studies of schoolpeople as Jonathan Messerli, *Horace Mann: A Biography* (New York: Alfred A. Knopf, 1972), Kathryn Kish Sklar, *Catharine Beecher: A Study in American Domesticity* (New Haven: Yale University Press, 1973), and Codman Hislop, *Eliphalet Nott* (Middletown, Conn.: Wesleyan University Press, 1971), but also in biographies like James Walter Fraser, "Pedagogue for God's Kingdom: Lyman Beecher and the Second Great Awakening" (unpublished doctoral thesis, Teachers College, Columbia University, 1975), Allen F. Davis, *American Heroine: The Life and Legend of Jane Addams* (New York: Oxford University Press, 1973), Harold Schwartz, *Samuel Gridley Howe: Social Reformer, 1801–1876* (Cambridge, Mass.: Harvard University Press, 1956), Mabel E. Talbot, *Édouard Seguin: A Study of an Educational Approach to the Treatment of Mentally Defective Children* (New York: Teachers College, Columbia University, 1964), Maurice F. Tauber, *Louis Round*

Wilson: Librarian and Administrator (New York: Columbia University Press, 1967), Joseph Cannon Bailey, *Seaman A. Knapp: Schoolmaster of American Agriculture* (New York: Columbia University Press, 1945), Glyndon Van Deusen, *Horace Greeley: Nineteenth-Century Crusader* (Philadelphia: University of Pennsylvania Press, 1953), Alexander Kendrick, *Prime Time: The Life of Edward R. Murrow* (Boston: Little, Brown and Company, 1969), and W. A. Swanberg, *Luce and His Empire* (New York: Charles Scribner's Sons, 1972). Even for the family, works like Charles Strickland, "A Transcendentalist Father: The Child-Rearing Practices of Bronson Alcott," *Perspectives in American History*, 3 (1969): 3–73, are invaluable. Additionally, group portraits from the several educative professions, such as Paul H. Mattingly, *The Classless Profession: American Schoolmen in the Nineteenth Century* (New York: New York University Press, 1975), Donna Merwick, *Boston Priests, 1848–1910: A Study of Social and Intellectual Change* (Cambridge, Mass.: Harvard University Press, 1973), and Bernard A. Weisberger, *The American Newspaperman* (Chicago: University of Chicago Press, 1961), are also useful.

There are two problems relating to the creation and use of these materials that are worthy of comment. First, in developing fresh monographs, particularly studies of realms other than the schools and colleges, the historian of education will generally find himself engaged in a twofold task, first, asking explicitly educational questions of documents long used for other purposes and, second, turning up new documents that will answer such explicitly educational questions. Thus, to cite a few examples, Douglas Sloan, in *The Great Awakening and Ameri-*

can Education: A Documentary History (New York: Teachers College Press, 1973), approached the eighteenth-century revivals from a fresh perspective, conceiving them not solely or even primarily as a religious movement but rather as an educational movement. This interpretation led him to include a number of documents well known to students of eighteenth-century religion, for example, Gilbert Tennent, *The Danger of an Unconverted Ministry* (Philadelphia: Benjamin Franklin, 1740) and Jonathan Edwards, *A Treatise Concerning Religious Affections* (Boston: S. Kneeland and T. Green, 1746), but to raise essentially educational questions of these documents, namely: How did the New Light ministers teach? What if anything was common to their pedagogy? What outcomes did they seek in the members of their congregations as a result of their instruction? And it led him also to include other documents less familiar to students of eighteenth-century religion but nevertheless helpful in illuminating basic educational issues, for example, a 1751 letter of Samuel Davies describing the "reading revivals" in Hanover County, Virginia, and a 1780 memoir by one of Francis Alison's students describing the course of study and methods of instruction in Alison's New London academy during the 1740s. In similar fashion, James Walter Fraser, in "Pedagogue for God's Kingdom," considered a familiar figure in nineteenth-century religious history but explicated his role as educator, demonstrating how Lyman Beecher self-consciously used the church, the school, the college, the theological seminary, the voluntary association, and the magazine as agencies for the systematic instruction of the public in a particular view of America and its destiny. If nothing else, the Sloan and Fraser volumes render Gilbert Tennent, Jonathan Edwards, Samuel Davies, Francis Alison, and Lyman Beecher significant figures in the history of American education.

A second problem concerns the use of extant monographs. Historians of education will frequently find themselves undertaking secondary analysis of studies initially written for quite different purposes and addressed to quite different questions from their own. (I am using the phrase "secondary analysis" here in the way social scientists use it in referring to the re-analysis of data originally gathered for other purposes.) Thus, for example, a monograph about the seventeenth-century church will go on for pages about the controversy over infant baptism, a matter of profound significance to students of theology but of only passing concern to students of education; while a monograph about the nineteenth-century newspaper will deal at length with the technology of the rotary press, once again, a matter of great interest to students of journalism but of little consequence to students of education. Obversely, the historian of education will have significant questions about the seventeenth-century church and the nineteenth-century newspaper that simply will never have occurred to students of those institutions per se. The task of the educational historian is clearly to mine these monographs and the sources on which they are based, using explicitly stated and critically analyzed theories of education, extracting what is valuable from their ore and then digging further in veins that may have been neglected. In the end, of course, there can be no substitute for fresh inquiries with educational questions uppermost in mind, but meanwhile there is much to be gained from secondary analysis of the extant literature.

I have noted here and elsewhere the tendency of educative institutions at particular times and places to relate to one another in configurations of education. As already mentioned, each of the institutions within a given configuration interacts with the others and with the larger society that sustains it and that is in turn affected by it. Configurations of education also interact, as configurations, with the society of which they are part. Thus, beyond the individual institutions of education, a new problematics for the history of education must concern itself with clusters, or constellations, or configurations of related institutions. The simplest illustrations derive from political or social movements that call upon a variety of educative agencies to advance their purposes. By way of example, John H. Calam, *Parsons and Pedagogues: The S.P.G. Adventure in American Education* (New York: Columbia University Press, 1971) deals with the cluster of educative institutions that incarnated the royalist program for colonies during the eighteenth century; Charles I. Foster, *An Errand of Mercy: The Evangelical United Front, 1790–1837* (Chapel Hill: University of North Carolina Press, 1960), T. Scott Miyakawa, *Protestants and Pioneers: Individualism and Conformity on the American Frontier* (Chicago: University of Chicago Press, 1964), and Walter Brownlow Posey, *Frontier Mission: A History of Religion West of the Southern Appalachians to 1861* (Lexington: University of Kentucky Press, 1966) deal with the clusters of educative institutions developed by popular religion during the nineteenth century; while Arthur A. Goren, *New York Jews*

and the *Quest for Community: The Kehillah Experiment,*
1908–1922 (New York: Columbia University Press, 1970)
deals with the cluster of educative institutions created by New
York's variegated Jewish population on the Lower East Side
during the early twentieth century. In quite different ways,
Joseph F. Kett, *The Formation of the American Medical Pro-*
fession: The Role of Institutions, 1870–1960 (New Haven: Yale
University Press, 1968) and Robert Stevens, "Two Cheers for
1870: The American Law School," *Perspectives in American*
History, 5 (1971): 403–548, deal with the clusters of schools
and professional societies that came into being at various stages
in the evolution of the learned professions in the United
States; Steven L. Schlossman, *Love and the American Delin-*
quent: The Theory and Practice of "Progressive" Juvenile Jus-
tice, 1825–1920 (Chicago: University of Chicago Press, 1977)
deals with the cluster of rehabilitative institutions developed in
the effort to curb juvenile delinquency; and Jane de Hart
Mathews, "Arts and the People: The New Deal Quest for a
Cultural Democracy," *Journal of American History,* 62
(1975): 316–339, deals with the cluster of educative institutions that the WPA Federal Arts Project employed in striving
for social justice through a program of cultural enrichment
called "Arts for the Millions."

At a more general level, the phenomenon of the educational configuration is illuminated by the study of communities—of the various ways in which communities educate so as
to perpetuate themselves and of the relationships among the
several educative institutions involved in the process. As in the
case of other aspects of the new problematics, the quickest

approach to these phenomena is through secondary analysis of extant community studies—of monographs such as Philip J. Greven, Jr., *Four Generations: Population, Land, and Family in Colonial Andover, Massachusetts* (Ithaca, N.Y.: Cornell University Press, 1970), Joseph E. Walker, *Hopewell Village: The Dynamics of a Nineteenth-Century Iron-Making Community* (Philadelphia: University of Pennsylvania Press, 1966), Merle Curti, *The Making of an American Community: A Case Study of Democracy in a Frontier Community* (Stanford, Calif.: Stanford University Press, 1959), Stephan Thernstrom, *Poverty and Progress: Social Mobility in a Nineteenth-Century City* (Cambridge, Mass.: Harvard University Press, 1964), and, among the best for the purpose, Robert S. Lynd and Helen Merrell Lynd, *Middletown: A Study in American Culture* (*New York: Harcourt, Brace and Company*, 1929) and *Middletown in Transition: A Study in Cultural Conflicts* (New York: Harcourt, Brace and Company, 1937). The problem is equally well illuminated by studies of distinct subcommunities, such as Kai T. Erikson, *Wayward Puritans: A Study in the Sociology of Deviance* (New York: John Wiley & Sons, 1966), John W. Blassingame, *The Slave Community: Plantation Life in the Ante-Bellum South* (New York: Oxford University Press, 1972), Moses Rischin, *The Promised City: New York's Jews, 1870–1914* (Cambridge, Mass.: Harvard University Press, 1962), and John A. Hostetler, *Hutterite Society* (Baltimore: Johns Hopkins University Press, 1974), and in particular by studies of utopian communities, for example, John F. C. Harrison, *Quest for the New Moral World: Robert Owen and the Owenites in Britain and America* (New York: Charles

Scribner's Sons, 1969) and Arthur Eugene Bestor, Jr., *Backwoods Utopias: The Sectarian and Owenite Phases of Communitarian Socialism in America, 1663–1829* (Philadelphia: University of Pennsylvania Press, 1950). The point bears repeating, of course, that secondary analysis of these community studies, like secondary analyses of the other literatures mentioned earlier, should be undertaken from the perspective of an explicit theory of education. And in this respect the Harrison and Bestor works, along with other studies of utopian ideals and communities, are especially relevant, since from *The Republic* down to *Walden II* there has been an educational theory at the heart of almost every major utopian proposal. In addition, the nature and character of the relationships among the several educative institutions within a particular community require careful scrutiny. In most of the literature to date, discussion of these relationships has been limited to passing remarks concerning identities or similarities with respect to the sponsorship, control, management, conduct, and clientele of the several institutions, and even these have been more often affirmed and assumed than explicated and specified.

III

THE OBVERSE of the configuration of education is the individual who comes to an educational situation with particular goals, needs, perceptions, sensibilities, and habits of learning; and a new problematics for the history of education must also concern itself with the ways in which different individuals have interacted with given configurations and with the diverse outcomes of those interactions. The initial key to such insights is the educational biography, a portrayal of an individual life focusing on the experience of education—the experience resulting from the deliberate, systematic, and sustained efforts of others to transmit or evoke knowledge, attitudes, values, skills, and sensibilities, as well as the experience involved in the subject's own deliberate, systematic, and sustained efforts to acquire knowledge, attitudes, values, skills, and sensibilities. An educational biography will generally begin with the efforts of others (parents, kin, peers, clergymen, schoolteachers) to nurture certain attitudes and behaviors and to teach certain knowledge and values, and with the subject's response to those efforts, which leads on the one hand to certain selective accommodations and patterns of believing, knowing, and doing, and on the other hand to an inevitable impact on those undertaking the nurturing and teaching. An educational biographer will ordinarily seek to discern in the maturing individual what Hope Jensen Leichter has called an "educative style," a set of characteristic ways of engaging in, moving through, and combining educational experiences. The chief situations and interactions in which an educative style is learned and relearned over time, as well as the ways in which the subject manifests this style through "propriate striving," are the special domain of the educational biographer.

There are no published educational biographies that illustrate the genre precisely, though Ellen Condliffe Lagemann and Toni Thalenberg are at work on studies that may prove exemplary. The most interesting relevant monographs, each of which presents a number of brief life histories that resemble the genre but do not directly illustrate it, are Daniel H. Calhoun, *Professional Lives in America: Structure and Aspiration, 1750–1850* (Cambridge, Mass.: Harvard University Press, 1965) and Oscar Handlin and Mary F. Handlin, *Facing Life: Youth and the Family in American History* (Boston: Little, Brown and Company, 1971). As might be expected, given the centrality of both the ideal and the reality of self-education in American life, there are many general autobiographies and biographies that also resemble the genre—Benjamin Franklin's autobiography and Carl Van Doren's biography of Franklin are virtually paradigmatic—and, in this realm as in others, secondary analysis of the extant literature with an explicit theory of education in mind can prove invaluable. In this respect, Joan Dash, *A Life of One's Own*, which deals with the careers of Margaret Sanger, Edna St. Vincent Millay, and Maria Goeppert-Mayer, readily illustrates the potential fruitfulness of such analysis, not least for the fact that it deals with the role conflicts of gifted, educated women during the early twentieth century and thereby inevitably raises questions about education in general and self-education in particular.

Any given individual will approach a particular configuration of education with his own purposes, his own agenda, his own prior experience, and his own habits of learning. The result will surely be a unique interaction, the outcome of which cannot be predicted by looking at either the individual or the configuration in isolation. Yet, to assert the uniqueness of individual educative experience is in no way to deny the value of grouping biographies for purposes of analysis; and indeed this sort of grouping is at the heart of such prosopographical (collective biographical) studies as Clifford K. Shipton's analyses of Harvard alumni and James McLachlan's current work on Princeton alumni. Other relevant prosopographical studies include George W. Pierson, *The Education of American Leaders: Comparative Contributions of U.S. Colleges and Universities* (New York: Frederick A. Praeger, 1969), P. M. G. Harris, "The Social Origins of American Leaders: The Demographic Foundations," *Perspectives in American History*, 3 (1969): 157–344, Colin Bradley Burke, "The Quiet Influence: The American Colleges and Their Students, 1800–1860" (unpublished doctoral thesis, Washington University, 1973), and David F. Allmendinger, Jr., *Paupers and Scholars: The Transformation of Student Life in Nineteenth-Century New England* (New York: St. Martin's Press, 1975).

The gathering and analysis of survey data concerning the educational clienteles of prior eras is one of the principal methodological devices of the new history of education, and some of the work has been especially useful in illuminating not only the effects of education but also the relationships among educative institutions. For example, Selwyn K. Troen, "Popular Education in Nineteenth-Century St. Louis," *History of Education Quarterly*, 8 (1973): 23–41, derives, from census data and the annual statistics of the school system, the percentages of St. Louis children attending school or actively employed at each age between five and twenty, thereby establishing average ages for at least two critical transitions in the lives of children, the shift from household to household-with-school and the shift from household-with-school to household (albeit sometimes a different household)-with-work. In like manner, Carl F. Kaestle and Maris A. Vinovskis, "From Fireside to Factory: School Entry and School Leaving in Nineteenth-Century Massachusetts" (mimeographed, 1975) uses state and local school reports to derive similar averages for Massachusetts children. In quite different fashion, Richard J. Jensen and Mark Friedberger, *Education and Social Structure: An Historical Study of Iowa, 1870–1930* (Chicago: The Newberry Library, 1976) uses census data to trace the effects of family background on schooling and of schooling in turn on the socioeconomic status of several thousand Iowans during the last decades of the nineteenth and first decades of the twentieth centuries. Once one recognizes that "family background" serves as both a catchall and a surrogate for a variety of educative variables, including father's education and occupation, number of siblings in the family, and type of religious affiliation, it becomes clear that Jensen and Friedberger are addressing themselves essentially to the relationships among three primary educative settings—household, school, and work. Josef J. Barton, *Peasants and Strangers: Italians, Rumanians, and Slovaks in an American City, 1890–1950* (Cambridge, Mass.: Harvard University Press, 1975) undertakes much the same sort of analysis with respect to the immigrant population of Cleveland, though it specifies the relationships in even greater detail than the Jensen and Friedberger study. Thus, in examining intergenerational career mobility, Barton argues (p. 135):

The acquisition of an occupational role involved two stages: the transition from the status of the family to a certain level of educational achievement, and the step from a given educational category to an occupational status. The assertion, then, that education is an important means of mobility implies at least three things: first, that there is a strong connection between education and subsequent occupational status (that is, education determines occupation to a large extent); second, that there is a high rate of educational mobility, so that children coming from different social strata have about the same chance of reaching various educational levels; and third, that there are no appreciable delay effects of the father's status on the son's career, in the sense that the father's status exerts little impact on the son's choice of occupation beyond its influence on education. The isolation of these three processes allows one to examine in some detail the actual pattern of education and mobility in immigrant families.

Again, if one translates "status of the family" into educational terms, Barton's study also becomes an analysis of the interaction among the several principal educative settings—household, school, and work. Of course, one is still left with the problem of disaggregating (or, even more fundamentally, of separating out via quite different methods, some of them nonstatistical) the many particular educative relationships involved both within and across these several institutions; but that problem is less susceptible to solution by multivariate analysis of survey data. One notes the contrast in perusing Horace Mann Bond, *Black American Scholars: A Study of Their Beginnings* (Detroit: Balamp Publishing, 1972), which uses survey data but then proceeds to deal with them through network-charting rather than multivariate analysis. In the end, the answer lies in using each of the several methods maximally and complementarily. No single biography will ever justify the level of confidence with respect to certain sorts of generalization that can be derived from survey data; conversely, no survey will ever offer the richness of detail that can be gleaned from such studies as Robert Manson Myers, ed., *The Children of Pride: A True Story of Georgia and the Civil War* (New Haven: Yale University Press, 1972) and its sequel, *A Georgian at Princeton* (New York: Harcourt, Brace, Jovanovich, 1976).

One of the more useful devices for the grouping of biographies in the recent literature has been the concept of "the generation," a concept that is inherently relevant since it rests on an assumption not merely of similar biological and even biographical determinants but also of a common world view— or, in educational terms, a common decisive educative experience. Thus, Stanley Elkins and Eric McKitrick, *The Founding Fathers: Young Men of the Revolution* (Washington, D.C.: American Historical Association, 1962), Gordon Wood, *The Creation of the American Republic, 1776–1789* (Chapel Hill: University of North Carolina Press, 1969), and Steven J. Novak, "The Rights of Youth: American Colleges and Student Revolt, 1789–1815" (unpublished doctoral thesis, University of California, Berkeley, 1974), for example, explicate the common *Weltanschauungen* of the Revolutionary and post-Revolutionary generations and their bearing on the education of those generations; a book such as Nathan Irvin Huggins, *Harlem Renaissance* (New York: Oxford University Press, 1971) uses "the generation" to suggest the mutual education of the Harlem community during the decades following World War I; and much of the recent literature on the history of student unrest, like Seymour Martin Lipset and Gerald M. Schaflander, *Passion and Politics: Student Activism in America* (Boston: Little, Brown and Company, 1971), employs as a basic model the "conflict of generations," a concept elucidated most fully in Lewis S. Feuer, *The Conflict of Generations: The Character and Significance of Student Movements* (New York: Basic Books, 1969).

Finally, there is the idea of "national character," which patently incorporates, *inter alia*, a notion of the generalized results of deliberate and systematic nurture. Thus, for example, monographs as different as David Riesman, Reuel Denney, and Nathan Glazer, *The Lonely Crowd: A Study of the Changing American Character* (New Haven: Yale University Press, 1950), David M. Potter, *People of Plenty: Economic Abundance and the American Character* (Chicago: University of Chicago Press, 1954), Daniel R. Miller and Guy E. Swanson, *The Changing American Parent: A Study in the Detroit Area* (New York: John Wiley & Sons, 1958), Clyde Kluckhohn, "Have There Been Discernible Shifts in American Values During the Past Generation?" in Elting E. Morison, ed., *The American Style: Essays in Value and Performance* (New York: Harper & Brothers, 1958), Richard L. Bushman, *From Puritan to Yankee: Character and the Social Order in Connecticut, 1690–1765* (Cambridge, Mass.: Harvard University Press, 1967), and Richard D. Brown, "Modernization and the Modern Personality in Early America, 1600–1865: A Sketch of a Synthesis," *Journal of Interdisciplinary History*, 2 (1971–72): 201–228, delineate changes in the American character over time and explore the sources and dynamics of these changes, among them, education. And inasmuch as self-instruction has constituted a good deal of this education, studies of popular literature, such as John G. Cawelti, *Apostles of the Self-Made Man* (Chicago: University of Chicago Press, 1965) and Richard Weiss, *The American Myth of Success: From Horatio Alger to Norman Vincent Peale* (New York: Basic Books, 1969), or of popular role models, such as Andrew Sinclair, *The Better Half: The Emancipation of American Women* (New York: Harper & Row, 1965), are also invaluable.

IV

IF THE PROCESS of education is indeed a series of transactions between an individual with a particular life history and institutions of education that tend to relate to each other in configurations, then the nature of the transactions themselves must also be at the heart of a new problematics for the history of education. Here, as elsewhere, the ideal study would be one that approaches the interactions between particular individuals and groups of individuals and specific configurations of education, with their "educationally significant others," from the perspective of an explicit theory of education. One such work is Thomas Lane Webber, "The Education of the Slave Quarter Community: White Teaching and Black Learning on the Ante-Bellum Plantation" (unpublished doctoral thesis, Teachers College, Columbia University, 1975), which defines education as "the knowledge, attitudes, values, skills, and sensibilities which an individual, or a group, consciously or unconsciously, has internalized" (p. 2), and which rests heavily, though not exclusively, on slave narratives. Webber concludes that however insistently white teachers, via household, church, and apprenticeship, attempted to inculcate notions of white supremacy, black inferiority, and the justice of slavery, the educational configuration of the quarter-community (including the black household, the black peer group, and the black clandestine congregation), teaching the values of black folklore, among other things, managed to keep alive contradictory notions of black equality and opposition to slavery, as well as the promise of ultimate justice.

Webber used a precise definition of education for his study, and, though I would criticize that definition as being overly latitudinarian, he clearly approached the primary source material with an explicit educational theory in mind. There are, of course, substantial literatures that treat other educational problems, employing more general theories of learning, socialization, enculturation, and acculturation. The typical "uses" of learning theory consist in applying to complicated phenomena simple notions of one-to-one correspondence, essentially in commonsense terms. Thus, a good deal of the traditional work conceives of the school as the sole educator and the student as some kind of tabula rasa, and then goes on to imply that schoolbooks embody the essence of schooling, so that once the content of the schoolbooks has been ascertained the effects of schooling can be deduced. Mark Sullivan assumed as much in the second volume of *Our Times: The United States, 1900–1925* (New York: Charles Scribner's Sons, 1927), subtitled *America Finding Herself*, where he located the sources of

American values on the eve of World War I between the covers of the McGuffey readers. And I assumed as much in *The American Common School: An Historic Conception* (New York: Teachers College, Columbia University, 1951), where I inferred the essence of a nineteenth-century public-school education from readers, spellers, geographies, and arithmetics. It is instructive to contrast these two analyses with the much richer and more complex picture given by Barbara Joan Finkelstein in her anthology of nineteenth-century description and reminiscence entitled "Governing the Young: Teacher Behavior in American Primary Schools, 1820–1880: A Documentary History" (unpublished doctoral thesis, Teachers College, Columbia University, 1970).

A more recent application of the notion of correspondence—this one in social terms—has appeared in Marxian analyses of the history of education, for example, Samuel Bowles and Herbert Gintis, *Schooling in Capitalist America: Educational Reform and the Contradictions of Economic Life* (New York: Basic Books, 1976), which draws inferences on the basis of similarities between the organization of education and the organization of production, assuming that the educational system helps integrate youth into the economic system "through a structural correspondence between its social relations and those of production" (p. 131). Once again, the correspondence tends to be asserted rather than demonstrated, and, apart from the similarity, nothing of its nature is elucidated.

A number of historians have drawn upon modern behavioral science theories in attempting to develop a more sophisticated understanding of educational transactions. Thus, for example, John Demos, *A Little Commonwealth*, uses psycho-analytical development theory in explicating the life cycle of individuals in colonial Plymouth. John W. Blassingame, *The Slave Community*, relies heavily on role theory in ascertaining the effects of the various components that constituted the educational configuration of the ante-bellum quarter-community. John A. Hostetler draws extensively on both socialization theory and enculturation theory in *Hutterite Society*, insisting that the society as a whole has served essentially as a school and that the Hutterite school has in the last analysis been a microsociety. And Robert F. Berkhofer, Jr., *Salvation and the Savage* and James Axtell, *The School upon a Hill: Education and Society in Colonial New England* (New Haven: Yale University Press, 1974) skillfully utilize acculturation theory to explain both the confrontation of two profoundly different configurations of education, the Anglo-American Christian and the Amerindian, and the role conflict engendered by the movement of individuals from one society to the other. To the extent that educational historians insist upon the very real distinctions among education, socialization, enculturation, and acculturation, they must, yet again, undertake secondary analyses of these studies and others like them if they would derive truly fundamental illumination of the educative process as it proceeded in former times. The caveat is worth reiterating: in the last analysis, there is no substitute for an explicit theory of education in the development of an adequate historiography of education.

Studies of national character, as suggested earlier, are useful for generalizing about the outcomes of education; and, as such, they may also help in illuminating the impact of education on society. Given the difficulty of separating the results of education from the results of other influences, however, the question of societal outcome will doubtless prove the most challenging aspect of a new problematics for the history of education. A number of inquiries in recent years have addressed themselves to the question. One line of work, exemplified by Kenneth A. Lockridge, *Literacy in Colonial New England: An Enquiry into the Social Context of Literacy in the Early Modern West* (New York: W. W. Norton & Company, 1974), has investigated the specific relationship between education and literacy as well as the relationship between literacy and the broader phenomenon of development, or modernization. Another line of work, exemplified by Richard J. Jensen and Mark Friedberger, *Education and Social Structure* and Samuel Bowles and Herbert Gintis, *Schooling in Capitalist America*, has investigated the relationship of familial and school education to social mobility in particular and to social and economic equality in general. Yet another line of work, flowing from the several essays reprinted in Theodore W. Schultz, *Investment in Human Capital: The Role of Education and of Research* (New York: The Free Press, 1971) and exemplified by Gary S. Becker, *Human Capital: A Theoretical and Empirical Analysis, with Special Reference to Education* (New York: National Bureau of Economic Research, 1964), investigates the relationship between investment in education and economic growth. And still another line of work, exemplified by the studies of Timothy L. Smith and his students—Timothy L. Smith, "Immigrant Social Aspirations and American Education, 1880–1930," *American Quarterly*, 21 (1969): 523–543, Josef J. Barton, *Peasants and Strangers*, and John Walker Briggs, "Italians in Italy and America: A Study of Change Within Continuity for Immigrants to Three American Cities, 1890–1930" (unpublished doctoral thesis, University of Minnesota, 1973)—investigates the role of education in the process of Americanization. And, most venturesome of all, Daniel L. Calhoun, *The Intelligence of a People* (Princeton, N.J.: Princeton University Press, 1973) investigates the role of education in the transformation of American intelligence during the nineteenth century, generalizing on the basis of evidence from the realms of teaching, shipbuilding, and bridgebuilding.

V

To define education as the deliberate, systematic, and sustained effort to transmit, evoke, or acquire knowledge, attitudes, values, skills, or sensibilities, is to leave ample room for mutual education across cultures, not only within the geographic boundaries of the United States (for example, between Anglo-Americans and Amerindians), but beyond those boundaries as well. Hence, a new problematics for the history of education must also concern itself with the deliberate import and export of cultural forms. In this realm, the historian of education has a rich recent literature on which to draw. To cite but several examples, Douglas Sloan, *The Scottish Enlightenment and the American College Ideal* (New York:

Teachers College Press, 1970) indicates the extent to which eighteenth-century Americans were profoundly influenced by and indeed deliberately drew upon Scottish forms and substance in developing provincial higher education. Gillian Lindt Gollin, *Moravians in Two Worlds: A Study of Changing Communities* (New York: Columbia University Press, 1967) traces the transplantation of a European configuration of education to the New World and the subsequent transformation of that configuration. John F. C. Harrison, *Quest for the New Moral World* is a paradigmatic study of the testing of European utopian thought in the American context, while Clifton Jackson Phillips, *Protestant America and the Pagan World: The First Half Century of the American Board of Commissioners for Foreign Missions, 1810–1860* (Cambridge, Mass.: Harvard University Press, 1969) is equally paradigmatic with respect to the export of American ideas to European and Asian settings. And Kenneth James King, *Pan-Africanism and Education: A Study of Race, Philanthropy, and Education in the Southern States of America and East Africa* (Oxford: Clarendon Press, 1971) explicates the way in which British colonial authorities during the early twentieth century took the American model of black vocational education, as developed at Tuskegee and Hampton institutes, and exported it to East Africa as an aspect of British colonial policy. These particular studies happen to deal with education, but the issues they raise concerning cultural import and export are generic. The phenomenon of cultural import is especially well elucidated in Bernard Bailyn, *The Ideological Origins of the American Revolution* (Cambridge, Mass.: Harvard University Press, 1967) and H.

Trevor Colbourn, *The Lamp of Experience: Whig History and the Intellectual Origins of the American Revolution* (Chapel Hill: University of North Carolina Press, 1965); the phenomenon of cultural export is especially well elucidated in Edward A. McCreary, *The Americanization of Europe: The Impact of Americans and American Business on the Uncommon Market* (Garden City, N.Y.: Doubleday & Company, 1964) and Carl J. Friedrich, *The Impact of American Constitutionalism Abroad* (Boston: Boston University Press, 1967).

VI

THE NEW HISTORY of education has tended to focus on the efforts of a variety of educative institutions, the results of those efforts in individual clients and groups of clients, and the nature and character of the transactions involved. In all of this, social history has been dominant. Yet, each of these dimensions has an obvious counterpart in intellectual history, for those who conduct educative institutions invariably have assumptions and aspirations about desirable outcomes and the most effective ways of achieving them, as do those who patronize those institutions. Consequently, there has emerged a new intellectual history addressed to the problems of education. One can cite, by way of example, studies as different as Rush Welter, *Popular Education and Democratic Thought in America* (New York: Columbia University Press, 1962), which is for all intents and purposes an intellectual history of American schooling, Merle Curti, *Human Nature and American*

Historical Thought (Columbia: University of Missouri Press, 1968) and John S. Haller, Jr., *Outcasts from Evolution: Scientific Attitudes of Racial Inferiority, 1859–1900* (Urbana: University of Illinois Press, 1971), which explore assumptions about human nature and educability, Maxine Greene, *The Public School and the Private Vision: A Search for America in Education and Literature* (New York: Random House, 1965), which discusses the profound differences in educational aspirations and assumptions on the part of writers and schoolmen in pre–Civil War New England, Linda K. Kerber, *Federalists in Dissent: Imagery and Ideology in Jeffersonian America* (Ithaca, N.Y.: Cornell University Press, 1970), which traces the Federalist and Republican modes of thought as they affected education in schools, colleges, and scientific academies, and John F. C. Harrison, *Quest for the New Moral World* and Laurence Veysey, *The Communal Experience*, which detail the impact of particular ideologies on modes of communal education. Needless to say, one aspect of this new intellectual history has been its sharp criticism of traditional views of particular educators and educative institutions, as witness Walter Feinberg, *Reason and Rhetoric: The Intellectual Foundations of 20th Century Liberal Educational Policy* (New York: John Wiley & Sons, 1975), Clarence J. Karier, Paul Violas, and Joel Spring, *Roots of Crisis: American Education in the Twentieth Century* (Chicago: Rand McNally & Company, 1973), and H. Shelton Smith, *In His Image, But . . . . : Racism in Southern Religion, 1780–1910* (Durham, N.C.: Duke University Press, 1972).

VII

THE LEITMOTIF of these observations has been that a clear, consistent, and precise theory of education is essential to any intelligent discussion of the problematics of the history of education. As John Herman Randall reminded us years ago, there is no such thing as history per se. Any history is always the history of something in particular, and the explanatory categories the historian uses in writing about that something in particular are almost invariably drawn from other domains—from politics or philosophy or psychology or economics, or from ordinary common sense. As soon as the historian attempts to go beyond mere chronicle, as soon as he seeks not only to arrange events in the order in which they occurred but also to explain how and why they occurred, as soon as he tries to view events in their multifarious relations, he must perforce reach beyond the events themselves to some set of laws, principles, or generalizations that will help make sense of them. And those laws, principles, or generalizations almost always come from outside the discipline of history. The argument put forward here has been essentially a particularization of Randall's: apart from some intelligent conception of education itself, there can be no truly intelligent conception of the history of education.

That said, it is perhaps important to make clear that the theoretical position I have taken is fundamentally interactionist, and is derived from George Herbert Mead and John Dewey in philosophy, Ruth Benedict and Ralph Linton in anthropology, Gordon Allport and Gardner Murphy in psychology, Talcott Parsons and Robert K. Merton in sociology, and Arthur F. Bentley and David B. Truman in political science, among others. From this interactionist view stems the definition of education as purposeful, the conception of the configuration as a patterning of institutions, the view of personality as a biosocial emergence, and the idea of the educative process as a continuum of contemporaneous and successive transactions. It might be noted, parenthetically, that interactionism is a characteristically American philosophy, forged in the crucible of the American experience. Almost a half-century ago, when the University of Paris conferred an honorary degree upon John Dewey, the citation referred to him, quite accurately, as "the most profound and complete expression of the American genius." However one judges the superlatives, the location of the man and his philosophy is incontrovertible.

Be that as it may, it should also be emphasized that the history presented here and the problematics it represents constitute only one set of possibilities among many. Depending on the particular theory of education that guides and informs the efforts of a particular historian, one history rather than another will result. But, given a multiplicity of theories and hence a variety of histories, the collective literature that emerges will surely be broader, richer, and in the end more profound than the simplistic accounts of an earlier era, which dealt solely with schools and colleges and tended to celebrate rather than investigate their accomplishments.

INDEX

165

Index

Baxter, Margaret, 73
Beaumont, Gustave de, 84
Becker, Gary S., 157
Beecher, Lyman, 141
Bender, Thomas, 58n
Benedict, Ruth, 162
Bennett, James Gordon, 44
Bentley, Arthur F., 163
Berkhofer, Robert F., Jr., 53n, 135
Bestor, Arthur Eugene, Jr., 145
Bible, 7, 10, 28
Blackburn, Gideon, 70
Blackburn University, 70, 86
blacks, 21, 22, 33, 52, 74–80, 114
Blassingame, John W., 80, 144
Bond, Horace Mann, 150
Book of Common Prayer, 7, 33
Boorstin, Daniel, 34
botanical garden (as educator), 55, 104, 115
Bowles, Samuel, 132, 155
Bridenbaugh, Carl, 4, 10
Briggs, John Walker, 158
Brown, Milton W., 120n
Brown, Richard D., 34, 152
Bryce-Laporte, R. S., 80n
Buddhists, 45
Burke, Colin Bradley, 148
Bushman, Richard L., 152
Bushnell, Horace, 91–92

Calam, John H., 142
Calhoun, Daniel H., 147, 158
camp meeting (as educator), 48, 63
catechism, 7
Cawelti, John G., 153
Centennial Exhibition (1876), 91
chautauqua, 104–105
Christians, 59
church (as educator): in colonial America, 15, 17, 28, 30, 38; in met-

ropolitan America, 99–100, 109; in national America, 48–49, 55, 56, 58–59, 63, 67–68; in Renaissance England, 7, 12–13
cinema (as educator), 105–106, 113
circus (as educator), 48
Clifford, Geraldine Jonçich, 134
Coburn, Frederick W., 57n
Cohen, Morris Raphael, 119
Coit, Stanton, 104
Colbourn, Trevor, 160
College of the City of New York, 54
College of New Jersey; see Princeton University
College of William and Mary, 18
Colman, Benjamin, 26
Columbia University, 115
Committees of Correspondence, 38
configuration of education: historiography of, 142–145; in colonial America, 19–22; in metropolitan America, 107–119; in national America, 55–70; in Renaissance England, 12–14
Confucians, 45
Congregationalists, 59, 68
Coolidge, John C., 58n
Cornell University, 102
Cotton, John, 10
Cremin, Lawrence A., viii, 155
Curti, Merle, vii, ix, 132, 144, 160–161

Dalzell, Robert F., Jr., 58n
dame school; see petty school
Dartmouth College, 31
Dash, Joan, 135, 147
Davidson, Chalmers Gaston, 62n
Davies, Samuel, 25, 140, 141
Davis, Allen F., 137, 138
Davis, Emerson, 53
demonstration farm, 105

166

Index

Demos, John, 137, 156
Denney, Reuel, 152
dental school, 54
Dewey, John, 94, 162, 163
didactic literature, 12, 14, 19, 56
Dilworth, Thomas, 36
domesticity, 46
Donne, John, 10
Dublin, Thomas, 61, 73
Dulany, Daniel, 71n
Dwight, Timothy, 43, 48

Eaton, Clement, 132
education: and freedom, 33, 37, 85–86, 121; as biography, 24–28, 71–83, 119–122, 145–153; as cultural export, 95–98, 158–160; as transaction, 153–158; configurations of, 12–14, 19–22, 55–70, 107–119, 142–145; definition of, viii, 134–136; in colonial New England, 19; in colonial New York, 20; in colonial Philadelphia, 20–21; in colonial Virginia, 19–20; in nineteenth-century Lowell, Mass., 58–61; in nineteenth-century Macoupin County, Ill., 67–71; in nineteenth-century Sumter District, S.C., 61–67; in twentieth-century Muncie, Ind., 108–110; in twentieth-century New York City, 113–119; of Abigail Adams, 26; of John Adams, 25; of Morris Raphael Cohen, 119; of Patrick Henry, 25; of Martha Jefferson, 26; of Thomas Jefferson, 25; of Lucy Larcom, 71–73; of Jacob Lawrence, 119–120; of Irving E. Lowery, 77–79; of James Henry Magee, 82; of John McAuley Palmer, 81–82; of Roger Sherman, 25; of Alfred E. Smith, 120–121; of Wilbur Smith, 121; of Jacob Stroyer, 74–77; of Jane Colman Turell, 26; of Mercy Otis Warren, 27

educational biography, 24–28, 71–83, 119–122, 145–153
educational transaction, 153–158
educative style, 9, 146
Edwards, Jonathan, 140, 141
Eggleston, Edward, 11
Elkins, Stanley, 151
Emmanuel College, 18
Emerson, Ralph Waldo, 72, 87
Episcopalians, 50, 63
Erikson, Kai T., 144
evangelicism (as pedagogy), 17, 48–49
Everett, Edward, 72
Exman, Eugene, 137
extracurricular activities, 100

factory (as educator), 60–61
family (as educator): in colonial America, 15, 16–17, 28; in metropolitan America, 98–99, 108–109, 111; in national America, 45–47, 55, 58; in Renaissance England, 8, 12
Farber, Bernard, 137
Feinberg, Walter, 132, 161
Fellman, David, ix
film (as educator); see cinema (as educator)
Finch College, 115
Finkelstein, Barbara Joan, 155
Flexner, Abraham, 102
Fordham University, 115
Foster, Charles I., 142
Franklin, Benjamin, 29, 122, 147
Fraser, James Walter, 138, 140, 141
freedom, 33, 37, 85–86, 121
Friedberger, Mark, 149
Friedrich, Carl J., 160
Frierson, John, 77–79

General Education Board, 101
generations, 151–152

Index

Genovese, Eugene D., 80
Gintis, Herbert, 132, 155
Gladden, Washington, 94
Glazer, Nathan, 152
Goeppert-Mayer, Maria, 135, 147
Gollin, Gillian Lindt, 159
Goody, Jack, 34n
Goren, Arthur A., 142–143
Graham, Patricia Albjerg, 136
Gray, Robert, 10
Greathouse, John S., 81
Greeley, Horace, 70
Greene, Maxine, 161
Gregorie, Anne King, 62n
Greven, Philip J., Jr., 15, 16, 144
guarded education, 20–21

Hall, David D., 137
Haller, John S., Jr., 161
Hamerow, Theodore S., ix
Hamilton, Milton W., 70n
Handlin, Mary F., 147
Handlin, Oscar, 121n, 135, 147
Harris, P. M. G., 148
Harrison, John F. C., 84, 144–145, 159, 161
Harvard College, 15, 18, 20, 31, 86
Hayes, Rutherford B., 87
Henry, Patrick, 25
Henry, Sarah, 26
Herbst, Jurgen, ix, 18n
higher education: in colonial America, 15, 18, 38; in metropolitan America, 101–102, 115; in national America, 53–55, 70; in Renaissance England, 7, 13–14
Hislop, Codman, 138
home-demonstration agent, 105
Hoover, Herbert, 126
Hostetler, John A., 144
household (as educator); see family (as educator)

Howard University, 54, 55
Huggins, Nathan Irvin, 151

illiteracy; see literacy
immigrants, 6, 24, 44, 45, 67, 98–99, 114
Indians, 5, 21–22, 33, 52–53
Inns of Court, 7, 13

Jackson, Sidney L., 132
Jefferson, Martha, 26
Jefferson, Thomas, 25
Jenkins, James, 63
Jensen, Richard J., 149
Jews, 6, 100, 114
Johnson, Edward, 23
Johnston, James, 31
Jones, Thomas, 38n
Juilliard School of Music, 115
juvenile court (as educator), 104

Kaestle, Carl F., ix, 36, 136, 149
Karier, Clarence J., 161
Kasson, John F., 61n
Katz, Michael B., 131, 133–134
Keayne, Robert, 22
Kendrick, Alexander, 139
Kennedy, John F., 100
Kerber, Linda K., 161
Kerlinger, Fred, 133
Kett, Joseph, 143
kindergarten, 97
King, Kenneth James, 96, 159
Kluckhohn, Clyde, 152
Kutler, Stanley I., ix

Lagemann, Ellen Condliffe, ix, 146
Larcom, Lucy, 71–73, 80, 86
law school, 53, 54, 101–102

168

Index

Index

Index

171

Index

West, E. G., 84
Whitehead, John S., 136
Whittaker, Jeremiah, 3
Winthrop, John, 10
women's education, 29, 53, 112
work (as education), 46, 102–103
Wright, Mary Byram, 68

Yale College, 38
Yeshiva College, 115
Young, H. Edwin, ix

zoological institute (as educator), 115